Scott Foresman

Editorial Offices: Glenview, Illinois • Parsippany, New Jersey • New York, New York
Sales Offices: Parsippany, New Jersey • Duluth, Georgia • Glenview, Illinois
Coppell, Texas • Ontario, California

Credits

Illustrations

Elizabeth Allen: pp. 57, 58, 63, 64, 73, 74, 76, 79, 80, 89, 90, 92, 95, 96; **Joe Bartos:** pp. 2, 66; **Maryjane Begin:** cover; **Penny Carter:** pp. 3, 4, 5, 6, 7, 8, 19, 20, 21, 22, 23, 24; **Eldon Doty:** pp. 40, 69, 70, 71, 72, 83, 84, 85, 86, 87, 88, 91, 97; **Ruth J. Flanagan:** pp. 12, 44, 60, 98–108; **Rachel Geswaldo:** pp. 18, 66; **Tim Haggerty:** p. 34; **Jennifer Beck Harris:** pp. 35, 36, 37, 39, 51, 52, 53, 54, 55, 56, 67, 68; **Olga Jakim:** p. 82; **Kersti Mack:** p. 50; **Patrick Merrell:** pp. 13, 29, 45, 61, 77, 93; **Albert Molnar:** p. 66; **Pattie Silver:** pp. 9, 10, 11, 15, 16, 25, 26, 28, 31, 32, 41, 42, 43, 47, 48

ISBN 0-328-02241-1

ISBN 0-328-04045-2

9 10-VO14-10 09 08 07 06 05 04

6 7 8 9 10-VO14-10 09 08 07 06 05 04

Table of Contents

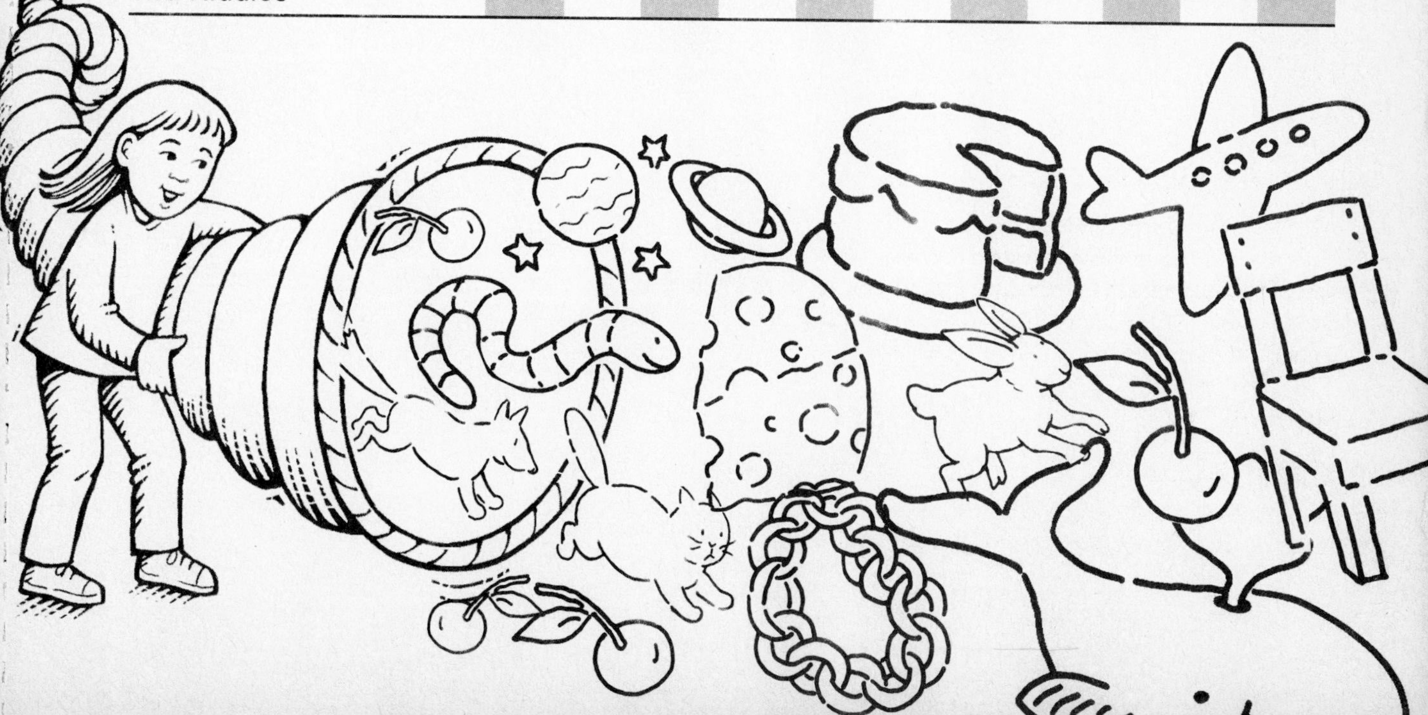

You *are* your child's first *and* best teacher!

Here are ways to help your child practice skills while having fun!

Day 1 Write a simple long *a* word that follows a consonant-vowel-consonant-*e* pattern, such as *cake* or *tale.* Have your child think of rhyming words that follow this pattern.

Day 2 Ask your child to write or say a short story that uses any of the following words that your child is learning to read: *after, as, call, laugh, something.*

Day 3 After you read a story to your child, ask your child to tell you which things in the story could really happen and which things are make-believe.

Day 4 Your child is practicing his or her listening skills. Read a short paragraph or story to your child. Challenge him or her to retell the key parts of the material read.

Day 5 Show your child some photographs or magazine cutouts of people in action. Help your child write or say a sentence to describe what the people are doing.

Read with your child EVERY DAY!

(fold here)

Family Times

The Red Stone Game **The Gingerbread Man**

Nate

We have a friend . . .
He likes to bake . . .
His name is Nate . . .
He made a cake . . .

Nate gave us cake . . .
On a cake plate . . .
It was so good . . .
We ate and ate . . .

Then we cleaned up . . .
We washed our plates . . .
We walked right out . . .
The big red gate . . .

This rhyme includes words your child is working with in school: words with the long *a* sound that end in *e (Nate, bake, made)* and words that end in *-ed (cleaned, walked)*. Chant "Nate" with your child. Clap each time a long *a* word is said. Tap your feet for each word ending with *-ed.*

Name: ______________________

Three in a Row

Materials index cards, markers

Game Directions

1. Write the action words shown below on index cards. Use the gameboard to play tick-tack-toe.

2. One player draws Xs. The other draws Os.

3. Players take turns picking a card, reading the word aloud, and marking either an X or an O on the same word with an *-ed* ending on the gameboard.

4. The first player who gets three marks in a row wins!

Action Words
jump, look, want, call, laugh, wash, cook, wish, pick

jumped	looked	wanted
called	laughed	washed
cooked	wished	picked

Name ______________________________

Circle the word for each picture.

cake

1. 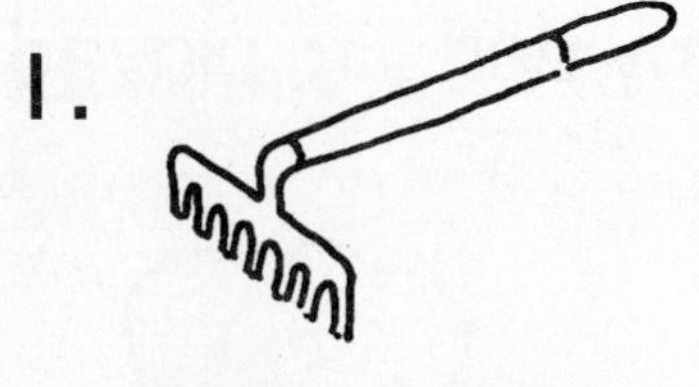
rake rack

2. 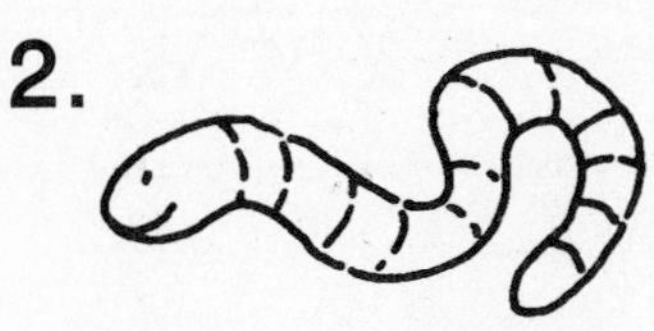
sneak snake

3. 
from frame

4. 
face fans

5. 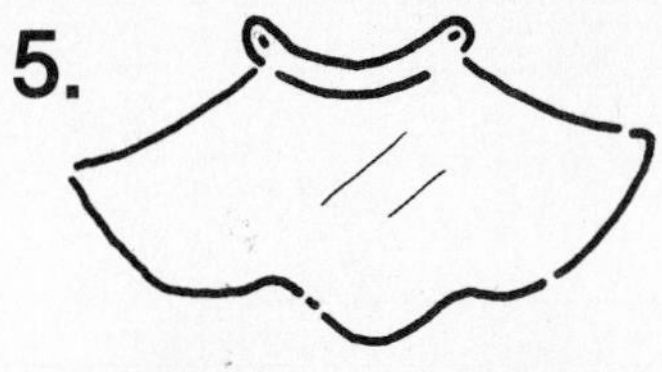
cape cap

6. 
plane plan

7. 
lock lake

8. 
tape tap

9. 
wave wove

10. 
scarf skate

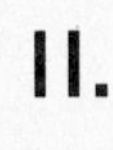

11. 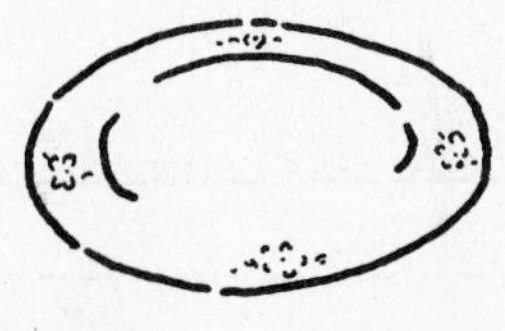
plate plum

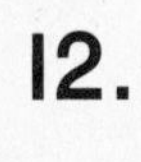

12. 
shapes shops

13. 
get gate

14. 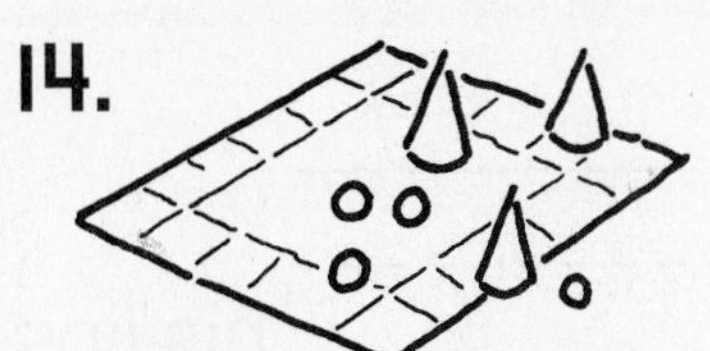
game gum

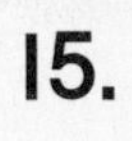

15. 
spice space

Notes for Home: Your child practiced reading words with the long *a* sound that follows a consonant-vowel-consonant-*e*, pattern such as *cake*. ***Home Activity:*** Work with your child to use each of the long *a* words shown in a sentence.

Name ______________________________

Add -ed to the word in ( ).
Write the new word on the line to finish the sentence.

Sunny and Jim play**ed**.

1. Sunny ______________________ Jim. (call)

2. She ______________________ to bake a cake. (want)

3. Jim ______________________ Sunny. (help)

4. The cake ______________________ good. (look)

5. Jim ______________________ his lips. (lick)

Notes for Home: Your child practiced writing words that end with *-ed*. ***Home Activity:*** Work with your child to write a story using the *-ed* words above.

Name ______________________________

Read each sentence.
Circle the picture that tells about the sentence.

after as call laugh something

1. Sam gave a call to Jane.

2. He ran after Jane.

3. Sam gave something to Jane.

4. Jane wanted to laugh.

5. It looked the same as Jane.

Notes for Home: This week your child learned to read the words *after*, *as*, *call*, *laugh*, and *something*. ***Home Activity:*** Write each word in a simple sentence. Ask your child to read the sentences to you.

Name ______________________________

Look at each pair of pictures.
Circle the picture that shows something that could really happen.
Write a sentence that tells about the picture you circled.

1.

____

2. ______________________________

3.

____

4. ______________________________

Draw a picture that shows something that could really happen.
Write a sentence that tells about the picture.

5.

____

____

Notes for Home: Your child made choices between events that could really happen and events that could not. ***Home Activity:*** Read a story with your child. Ask your child which parts of the story could really happen and which could not.

Name ______________________________

A **verb** is a word that can show action.
Waves is a verb.

Tom **waves** to Min.

Circle the verb in each sentence.
Draw a line from each sentence to the picture it matches.

1. The fox runs after the cat. 6. 

2. The cat jumps over the wall. 7. 

3. The fox stops at the wall. 8. 

4. The cat hops up on the wall. 9. 

5. The cat laughs. 10. 

Notes for Home: Your child circled verbs that show actions and matched each sentence to a picture. ***Home Activity:*** Together, write six verbs on separate slips of paper. Take turns. You or your child picks a slip and acts out the verb. The other guesses the action.

Name ______________________________

Pick a word from the box to finish each sentence.
Write it on the line.

after	as	call	catch	laugh	something

1. Ann runs ______________________ Nick.

2. But she is not as fast ______________________ he is.

3. Ann can't ______________________ him.

4. Ann can ______________________ Nick.

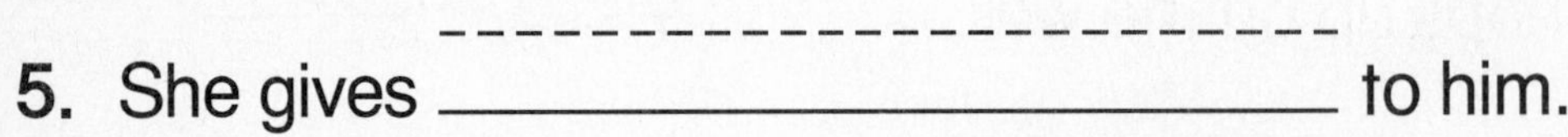

5. She gives ______________________ to him.

6. Now they ______________________ and eat.

Notes for Home: Your child completed sentences using newly learned words.
Home Activity: Work with your child to make up a story using as many of the words from the box as possible.

Name ______________________

cast

plant

hand

stump

Pick letters from the box to finish each word.
Write the letters on the line.

st nt nd mp

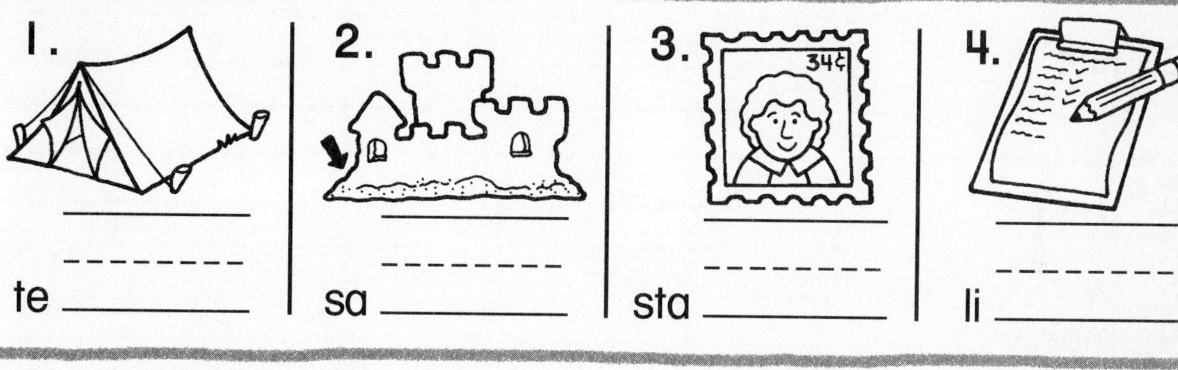

1. te ______
2. sa ______
3. sta ______
4. li ______

5. po ______
6. ju ______
7. ce ______
8. ne ______

Find the word that has the same ending sound as the picture.
Mark the ⬭ to show your answer.

9. ⬭ lamp
⬭ last
⬭ land

10. ⬭ stand
⬭ rent
⬭ rust

Notes for Home: Your child reviewed words with final consonant blends *st, nt, nd,* and *mp* such as *cast, plant, hand,* and *stump*. ***Home Activity:*** Pick one final consonant blend such as *st* or *nd*. Have your child name as many words ending with that sound as possible.

Name ______________________________

Look at each word. **Say** it.
Listen for the **long a** sound in  .

	Write each word.	**Check** it.
1. ate		
2. late		
3. gave		
4. make		
5. take		
6. bake		

Word Wall Words

Write each word.

7. as		
8. after		

Notes for Home: Your child learned to spell words with the long *a* sound heard in *cake*. ***Home Activity:*** Say each spelling word. Have your child use it in a sentence. Then say the spelling word again and have your child write it down.

Name ______________________

Read the sentence.
Underline the verb.
Write the verb on the line.

1. Dan bakes a cake.

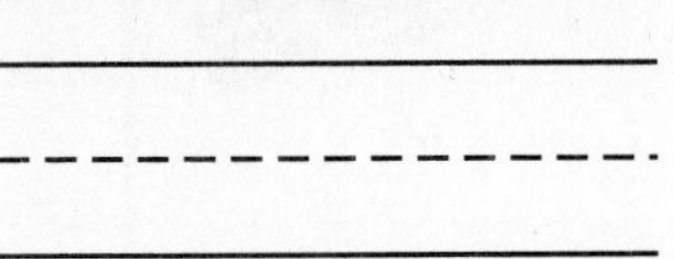

2. Mom eats the cake.

3. Dan calls Dad.

4. Dad runs home fast.

5. Dad asks for more!

Notes for Home: Your child identified and wrote verbs—words that show action. ***Home Activity:*** Read a story with your child. Ask your child to point out the verbs in the sentences. Later, make a list of some of the action words and take turns acting them out.

Name ______________________

Test-Taking Tips

1. Write your name on the test.
2. Read each question twice.
3. Read all the answer choices for the question.
4. Mark your answer carefully.
5. Check your answer.

Name ______________________

Part 1: Vocabulary

Read each sentence.
Mark the ⬭ for the word that fits.

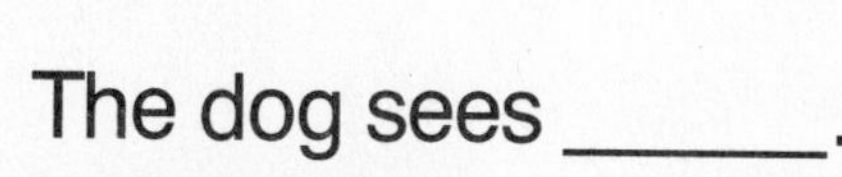

1. The dog sees ______.

⬭ laugh ⬭ know ⬭ something

2. The dog runs ______ the cat.

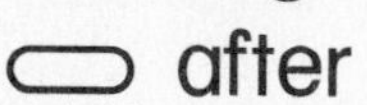

⬭ after ⬭ as ⬭ now

3. Now they ______ the dog.

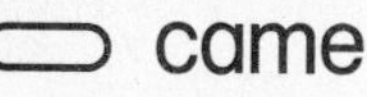
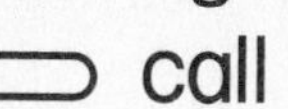
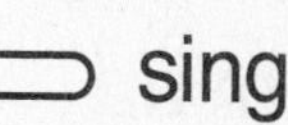

⬭ came ⬭ call ⬭ sing

4. They ______ at the dog.

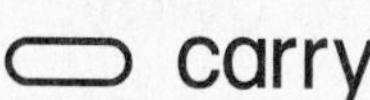

⬭ laugh ⬭ carry ⬭ hold

5. The dog did not ______ the cat.

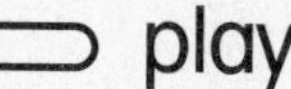

⬭ make ⬭ play ⬭ catch

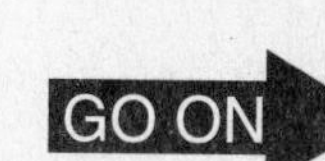

Name ______________________________

Part 2: Comprehension

Read each question.
Mark the ⬭ for the answer.

6. Who makes the Gingerbread Man?
   - ⬭ the man
   - ⬭ the woman
   - ⬭ the girl

7. What does the Gingerbread Man do first?
   - ⬭ runs from the farm
   - ⬭ sees some water
   - ⬭ takes a ride

8. Why does the Gingerbread Man laugh?
   - ⬭ No one can catch him.
   - ⬭ He wants to get wet.
   - ⬭ The fox is funny.

9. What does the Gingerbread Man think the fox will do?
   - ⬭ eat him up
   - ⬭ help him
   - ⬭ bring him water

10. What part of the story could be real?
    - ⬭ A gingerbread man runs away.
    - ⬭ A fox talks to a gingerbread man.
    - ⬭ A boy wants to eat a gingerbread man.

STOP

Name ____________________

Underline the word that has the same beginning sound as **gingerbread**.
Draw a line from the sentence to the picture it matches.

1. He ran in the gym.

5. 

2. The ring has a gem in it.

6. 

3. I saw a giraffe at the zoo.

7. 

4. Do not get his germs!

8. 

Find the word that matches each picture.
Mark the ⊂⊃ to show your answer.

9. 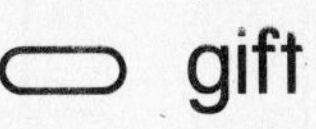
⊂⊃ giant
⊂⊃ gift
⊂⊃ gum

10. ⊂⊃ girl
⊂⊃ gerbil
⊂⊃ gas

Notes for Home: Your child reviewed the soft g sound heard in *gingerbread*. ***Home Activity:*** Play a game in which you describe a soft *g* word on this page and you ask your child to guess the word. For example: *This is an animal with a long neck. (a giraffe)*

Name ______________________

ate late gave make take bake

Pick a word from the box to finish each sentence.
Write it on the line. Use each word only once.
Hint: The word rhymes with the underlined word.

1. Did you ____________ my big, red <u>rake</u>?

2. I want to ____________ a yummy <u>cake</u>.

3. I sat on the <u>crate</u> as I ____________ .

4. I <u>hate</u> to be ____________ .

Pick a word from the box to match each clue.
Write it on the line.

5. It begins with **m**.

____

6. It rhymes with *cave*.

____

Pick a word from the box that fits in each puzzle.
Write it in the puzzle.

as after

7.				

8.	

Notes for Home: Your child practiced spelling words with long *a* that end in *e* and two frequently used words: *as, after. **Home Activity:*** Have your child tell a short story that uses the spelling words. Work together to write the story.

You *are* your child's first *and* best teacher!

Here are ways to help your child practice skills while having fun!

Day 1 Write a simple long *a* word that follows a consonant-vowel-consonant-*e* pattern, such as *lake* or *game*. Have your child name other long *a* words that rhyme with this word.

Day 2 Help your child write sentences that use the words that he or she is learning to read this week: *every, made, mother, of,* and *was.*

Day 3 After you read a story to your child, talk about things in his or her life that are similar to the story's characters or plot.

Day 4 Your child is learning about choral, or group, reading. Practice reading "We Took Our Family to the Lake," shown on page 1, individually and then together.

Day 5 Work with your child to name some verbs ending in *-s*. Then, have your child make up simple sentences using each verb along with the name of a family member, such as: *Dad sits. Jim runs.*

Read with your child EVERY DAY!

(fold here)

Family Times

The Same as You **Cherry Pies and Lullabies**

We Took Our Family to the Lake

We took our family to the lake.
We thought of things
That we could take.
We brought chicken and a
Chocolate cake.
We took our family to the lake.

We took the cake plates
That are blue.
We took the games
And checkers too.
We took the chairs.
We brought a few.
We took our family to the lake.

This rhyme includes words your child is working with in school: words with the long *a* sound that end with an *e (lake, take)* and words that begin with *ch (chicken, chairs)* and *th (thought, things)*. Make a list of the things the family took to the lake.

Name: ____________________

Coin Toss

Materials paper, marker, 1 coin

Game Directions

1. Make a large gameboard like the one shown.

2. Players take turns tossing the coin onto the gameboard and saying a word that begins with the letters shown in the square.

3. A correct answer earns the number of points shown in that square.

4. The first player to get 10 points wins!

ch 1	th 2	ch 3	th 1
th 2	ch 3	th 1	ch 2
ch 3	th 1	ch 2	th 3
th 1	ch 2	th 3	ch 1

Name ______________________________

Help Kate get to the lake.
Color each box that has the **long a** sound in **lake.**
Write each **long a** word you color on the line.

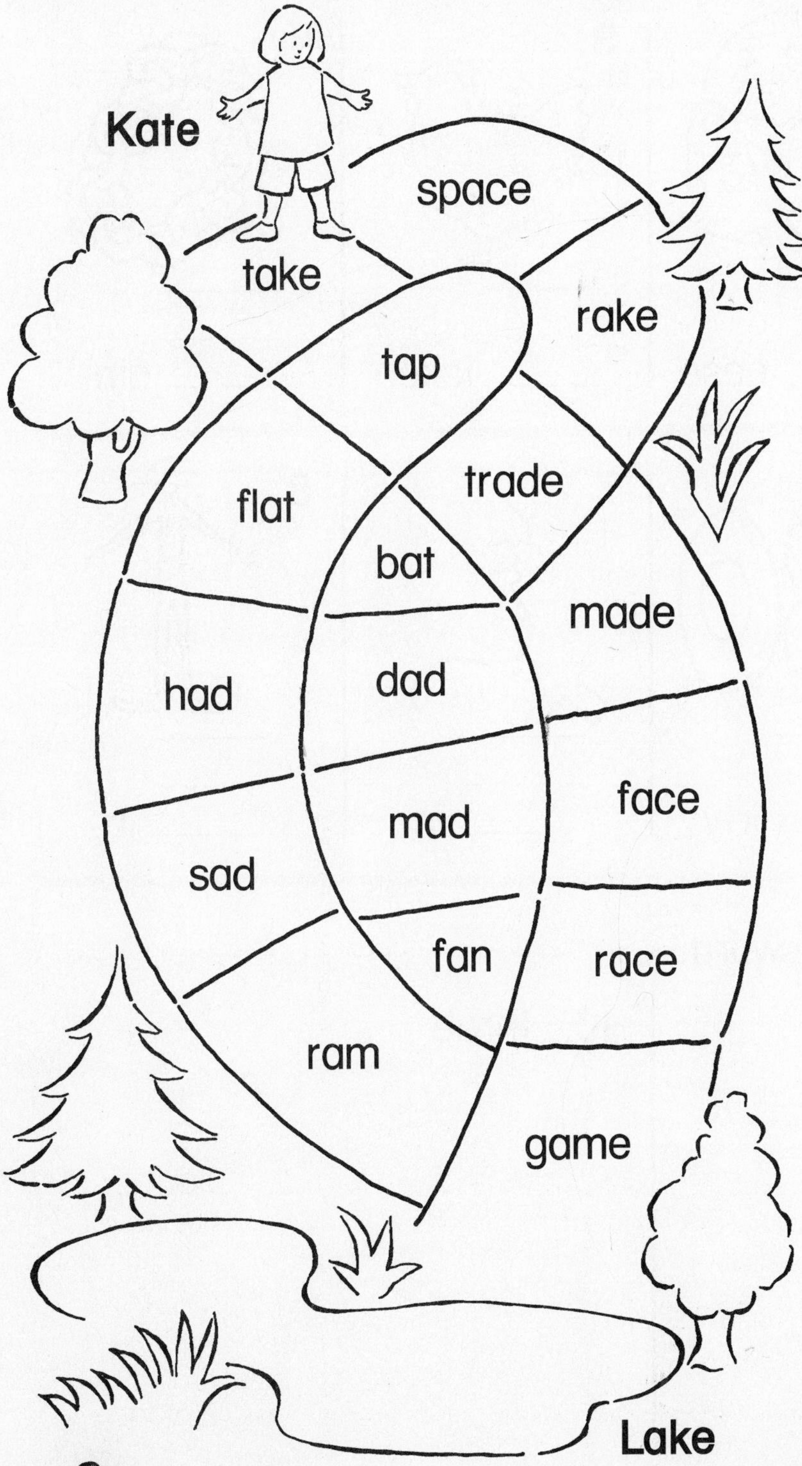

1. ______________
2. ______________
3. ______________
4. ______________
5. ______________
6. ______________
7. ______________
8. ______________

Notes for Home: Your child identified and wrote words with the long *a* sound that follow a consonant-vowel-consonant-*e* pattern, such as *lake*. ***Home Activity:*** Work with your child to name pairs of rhyming words that have the long *a* sound, such as *bake* and *take*.

Name ______________________________

Say the word for each picture.
Write ch or **th** to finish each word.

cherry thanks

1. ______ umb
2. ______ eese
3. ______ icken
4. ______ ain

5. ______ air
6. ______ irty
7. ______ in
8. ______ in

Draw a picture for each word.

9. children

10. three

Notes for Home: Your child added the initial digraphs *th* and *ch* (two letters that together stand for one sound) to complete words. ***Home Activity:*** Write down several words that begin with *ch* or *th*. Ask your child to read them to you.

Name ______________________

Pick a word from the box to finish each sentence.
Write it on the line.

every	made	mother	of	was

1. My mother ______________ me a doll.

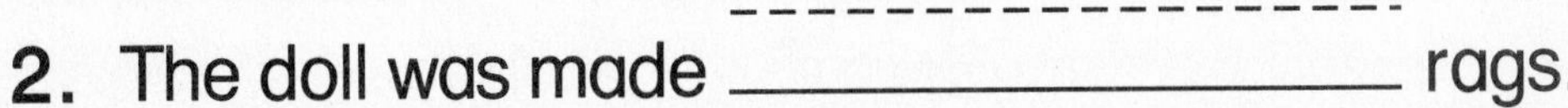

2. The doll was made ______________ rags.

3. It ______________ soft.

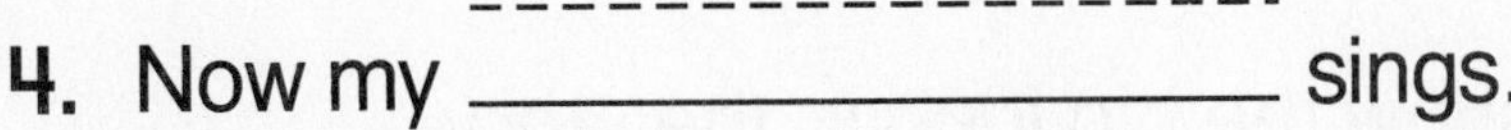

4. Now my ______________ sings.

5. She sings to us ______________ time we go to bed.

Notes for Home: This week your child learned to read the words *every*, *made*, *mother*, *of*, and *was*. ***Home Activity:*** Help your child write or tell you sentences that include these words.

Name ______________________________

Read the story.
Follow the directions below.

Fun at the Lake

John and his mom and dad like to go to the lake.
John swims. They all play ball.
They have many good things to eat.
They laugh and have a good time.
The lake is fun for them all.

1. Which sentence tells the big idea? Underline it.

   Moms, dads, and kids do things to have fun.
   John likes to swim.
   It is fun to eat good things.

2.-4. How did you know the big idea? Underline three sentences in the story that helped you know.

5. Draw a picture to show the big idea in the story.

Notes for Home: Your child identified a story's theme, or its big idea. ***Home Activity:*** Read a story with your child. Discuss the story's big idea. Help your child connect this idea to something in his or her own life.

Name ______________________________

A **verb** is a word that shows action.
Put an **-s** at the end of a verb if there is **one** person, animal, or thing doing the action.

Jake **plays** with a ball.

Add -s to each verb in ( ).
Write the new verb on the line to finish each sentence.

1. Jill ______________ to Bill. (wave)

2. Mike ______________ the big book. (read)

3. Nick ______________ the van. (see)

4. Nan ______________ her mother. (call)

5. Tom ______________ on the mat. (jump)

Draw a picture to show the action of one of the sentences above.

Notes for Home: Your child added *-s* to verbs with a singular subject (one person, place, or thing). ***Home Activity:*** Work with your child to write and illustrate a story about one boy or girl. Then ask your child to underline the verbs he or she uses.

Name ______________________

Pick a word from the box to finish each sentence.
Write it on the line.

every	made	mother	of	was

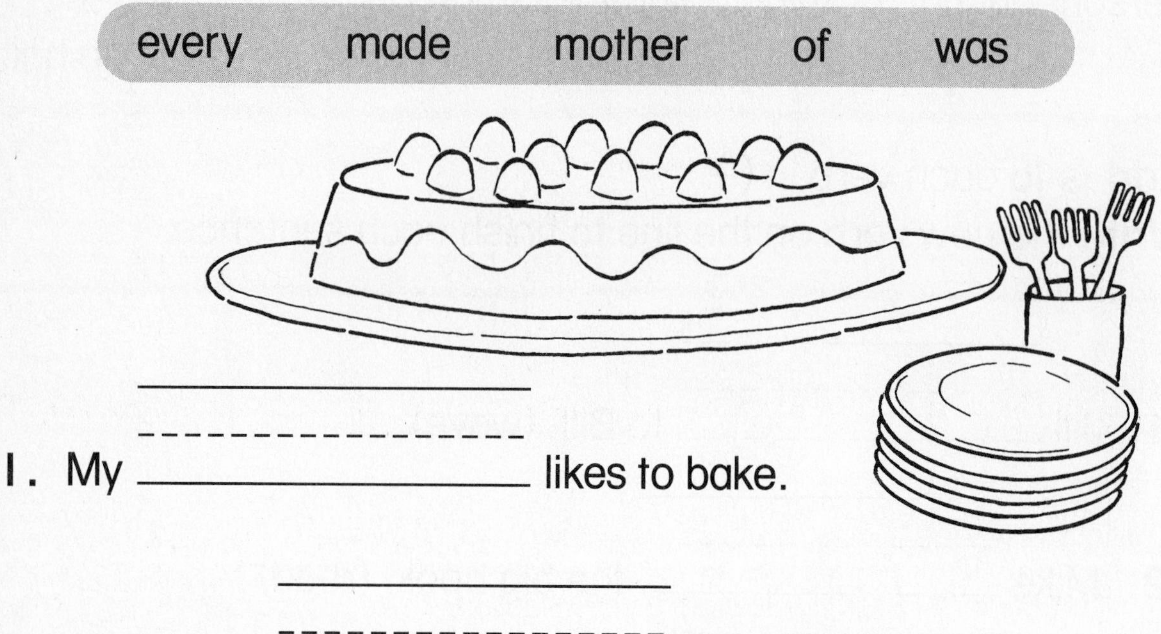

1. My ______________ likes to bake.

2. This is one ______________ her cakes.

3. ______________ cake she bakes is good!

4. Once she ______________ a pink cake.

5. It ______________ good.

Notes for Home: Your child completed sentences using words that he or she learned this week. ***Home Activity:*** Recall with your child a time when the two of you baked or cooked together. Work together to write sentences about it using as many of these words as possible.

Name ______________________________

Read the table of contents.
Write an answer to each question.

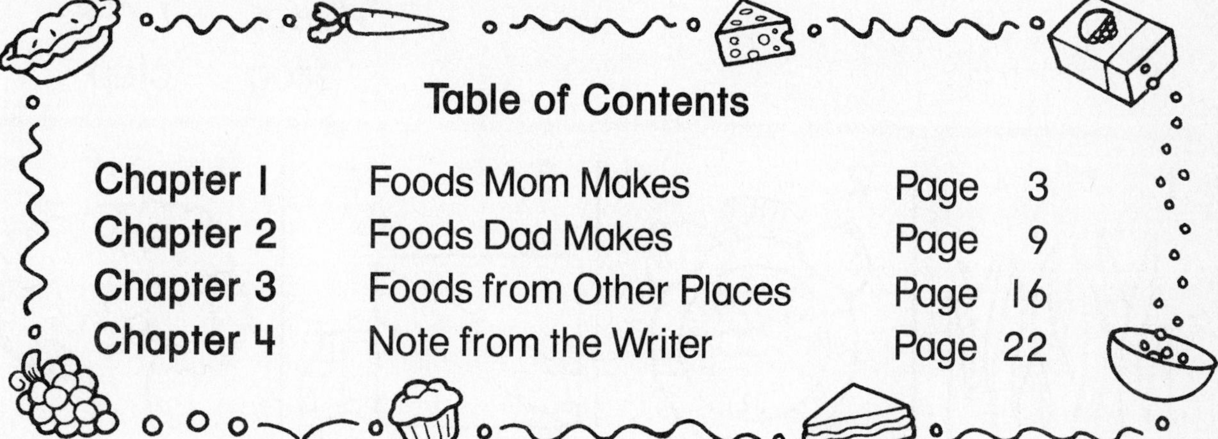

Table of Contents

1. How many chapters are in the book? ________

2. On what page does Chapter 1 start? ________

3. Which chapter comes after Foods Mom Makes?

____

4. On what page does Foods from Other Places start? ________

5. What is on page 22?

____

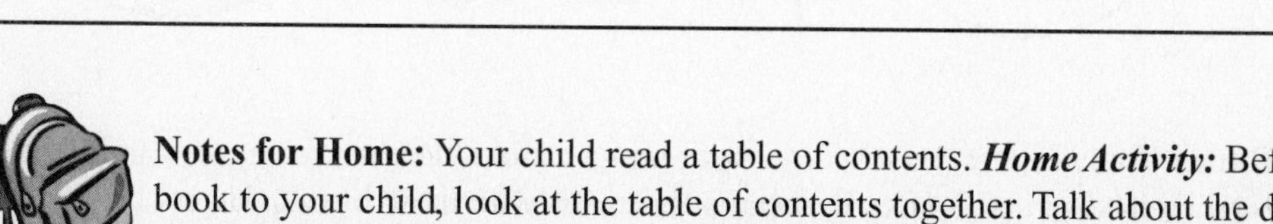

Notes for Home: Your child read a table of contents. ***Home Activity:*** Before you read a chapter book to your child, look at the table of contents together. Talk about the different chapter titles, the number of pages per chapter, and anything else listed in the table of contents.

Name ______________________________

Circle the word for each picture.

frog clap

1.

grass glass

2.

crack clock

3.

tuck truck

4.

tree tee

5.

tack track

6.

fog flag

7.

glad grapes

8.

crab claw

Find the word that has the same beginning sounds as the picture.
Mark the ⊂⊃ to show your answer.

9. ⊂⊃ club
⊂⊃ crib
⊂⊃ glad

10. ⊂⊃ dump
⊂⊃ dress
⊂⊃ doll

Notes for Home: Your child reviewed words with initial *r* and *l* blends, such as *frog* and *clap*. ***Home Activity:*** Help your child make flashcards for words with these blends. He or she can write the word on one side of a card and draw a picture to illustrate it on the other side.

Name ______________________________

Look at each word. **Say** it.
Listen for the **short a** or **long a** sound.

	Write each word.	**Check** it.
1. tap		
2. cap		
3. mad		
4. tape		
5. cape		
6. made		

Word Wall Words

Write each word.

7. of		
8. was		

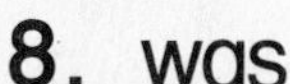

Notes for Home: Your child spelled words with the short *a* sound *(cap)* and the long *a* sound *(cape),* as well as two frequently used words: *of, was.* ***Home Activity:*** Read each word to your child. Have your child sort the words into short *a* words, long *a* words, and Word Wall Words.

Name ______________________

Circle the verb that tells what one person or animal does.
Write the verb on the line to finish each sentence.

reads   read

1. Mom ______________ a book.

sing   sings

2. Dad ______________ a song.

sleep   sleeps

3. Sally ______________ in her bed.

sits   sit

4. Skip ______________ by the bed.

nap   naps

5. Fluff ______________ on the bed.

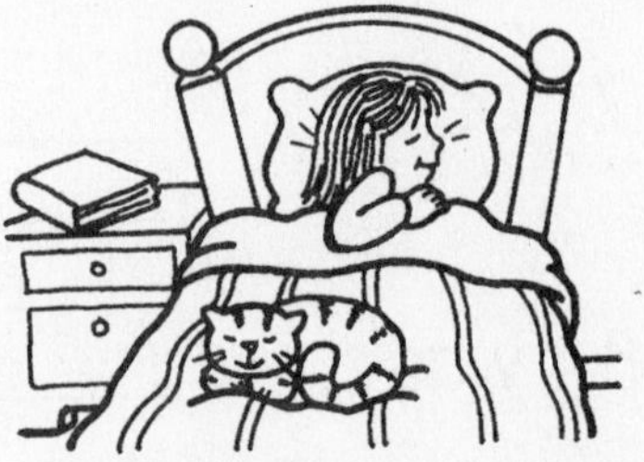

Notes for Home: Your child chose verbs to show the action of one person or animal. ***Home Activity:*** Have your child say a sentence about each of your family members. Ask your child to identify the verbs he or she uses in each sentence.

Name ______________________________

Part 1: Vocabulary

Read each sentence.
Mark the ⬭ for the word that fits.

1. Fran ______ a cake.

 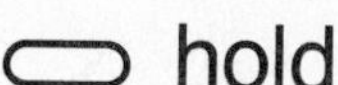

⬭ made ⬭ hold ⬭ said

2. "My _____ will like this," she said.

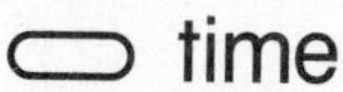

⬭ time ⬭ mother ⬭ who

3. Then it ______ time for bed.

⬭ was ⬭ call ⬭ made

4. Mom will read a lot ______ books.

⬭ some ⬭ of ⬭ all

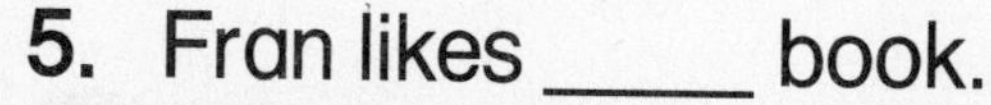

5. Fran likes _____ book.

⬭ for ⬭ as ⬭ every

GO ON

Name ________________________

Part 2: Comprehension

Read each question.

Mark the ⬭ for the answer.

6. What does the grandmother bake?
   - ⬭ cherry pie
   - ⬭ hot dogs
   - ⬭ plum pie

7. Who made a crown of flowers for the girl?
   - ⬭ her great-grandmother
   - ⬭ her grandmother
   - ⬭ her mother

8. Why does the mother give the girl a quilt?
   - ⬭ The girl asks for one.
   - ⬭ The mother had one when she was small.
   - ⬭ The grandmother tells the mother to.

9. Every woman in this story
   - ⬭ has a little girl.
   - ⬭ plants flowers.
   - ⬭ bakes all day.

10. In this story, every woman
    - ⬭ does the same things in her own way.
    - ⬭ has the same crown of flowers.
    - ⬭ lives in the same place.

STOP

Name ______________________________

Write qu to finish each word.
Draw a line from the word to the sentence where it belongs.

quilt

1. ________ iet
2. ________ iz
3. ________ estion
4. ________ een

5. The ______ has many rings.
6. Ned is sleeping. Please be ______ .
7. We had a math ______ today.
8. May I ask a ______ ?

Find the word that has the same beginning sound as 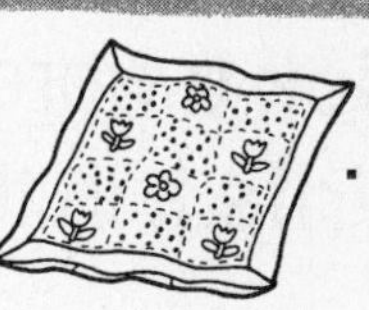 .
Mark the ⬭ to show your answer.

9. ⬭ gulp
   ⬭ quick
   ⬭ pick

10. ⬭ quit
    ⬭ grit
    ⬭ kit

Notes for Home: Your child reviewed the sound /kw/ that the letters *qu* represent as in *quilt*. ***Home Activity:*** Look in a dictionary to find simple words beginning with *qu* that your child will know. Give your child clues about the word's meaning and see if he or she can guess it.

Name ______________________

tap cap mad tape cape made

Write three words from the box that have a **short a** sound.

1. ____________ 2. ____________ 3. ____________

Write three words from the box that have a **long a** sound.

4. ____________ 5. ____________ 6. ____________

Pick a word from the box to finish each sentence.
Write it on the line.

7. He has a ____________ .

8. She has a ____________ .

Pick a word from the box that fits in each puzzle.
Write it in the puzzle.

of
was

9.		

10.	

Notes for Home: Your child practiced spelling words with short *a (tap)* and long *a (tape)*, as well as two frequently used words: *of, was.* ***Home Activity:*** Say each spelling word and use it in a sentence. Repeat the spelling word and have your child write it down.

You *are* your child's first *and* best teacher!

Here are ways to help your child practice skills while having fun!

Day 1 Draw pictures with your child of objects whose names have the long *o* sound that follow a consonant-vowel-consonant-*e* pattern as in *rose* or *bone.* Write a label for each picture.

Day 2 Ask your child to write or say aloud a thank-you note that uses any of the following words: *father, going, has, thank,* and *very.*

Day 3 Your child is learning about a story's main idea. The next time you are reading together, ask your child to tell what the story is all about in a sentence or two.

Day 4 Help your child write a family history that describes each family member.

Day 5 Ask your child to name some verbs. Then have him or her use them in sentences about more than one person in your family, such as: *Mom and I jump. We sing.*

(fold here)

Family Times

Rose and Grandma Make the Sun Shine **Our Family Get-Together**

Oh, Visit My Home

Oh, visit my home. It is shaped like a dome.
We can whistle and climb a tall rope.
We can pick a white rose.
We can find shells and doze.
We'll have fun when you visit. I hope.

Oh, visit my home.
We can look for tall ships and big whales.
We can see the white beach,
Or we might eat a peach.
We can sit on the wharf and tell tales.

This rhyme includes words your child is working with in school: words with the long *o* sound that end in *e (rope, home)* and words that begin with *sh (shells, ships)* and *wh (white, whales)*. Sing "Oh, Visit My Home" along with your child. Talk about all the fun things that can be done at your home.

Name: ______________________

Color the Flower

Materials red and blue crayons

Game Directions

1. One flower is marked *sh*. The other flower is marked *wh*. Take turns adding *sh* or *wh* to each flower petal.

2. If the word makes sense, color the petal blue.

3. If the word does not make sense, color the petal red.

Name ______________________

Pick the word with the **long o** sound to finish each sentence.
Write it on the line.

rope

home hot

1. Ben walked ______________ .

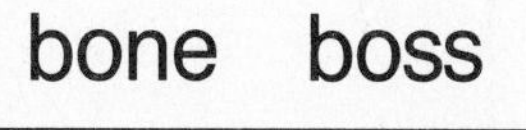

bone boss

2. Pug wants a ______________ .

stop stone

3. Hal picks up a ______________ .

joke job

4. I told my best ______________ .

not nose

5. Sal bumped her ______________ .

Notes for Home: Your child identified and wrote words with the long *o* sound that follow the pattern consonant-vowel-consonant-*e* (CVC*e*) as in *rope*. ***Home Activity:*** Work with your child to write a story using as many long *o* words that follow the CVC*e* pattern as possible.

Name ______________________________

Say the word for each picture.
Write sh or **wh** to finish each word.

<u>sh</u>irt <u>wh</u>eat

1. ________op

2. ________ip

3. ________eel

4. ________ale

5. ________isper

6. ________oe

7. ________iskers

8. ________eep

9. ________istle

10. ________ell

Notes for Home: Your child identified words that begin with *sh* and *wh* as in *<u>sh</u>irt* and *<u>wh</u>eat*. ***Home Activity:*** Write a list of words that begin with *sh* and *wh*. Help your child read the words aloud and draw pictures of them.

Name ______________________________

Pick a word from the box to finish each sentence.
Write it on the line.

father	going	has	thank	very

1. Jim walks with his ______________ .

2. They are ______________ to see Grandma.

3. Jim ______________ a cake for her.

4. He wants to ______________ her for the game she gave him.

5. He likes the game ______________ much.

Notes for Home: This week your child is learning to read the words *father, going, has, thank,* and *very*. ***Home Activity:*** Write simple sentences with these words. Help your child read the sentences aloud. Have your child point to the words he or she knows as you read.

Name ______________________________

Read the story.
Circle the sentence that tells what the story is all about.
Draw a picture that shows what the story is all about.

1. Everyone came to my home.
Bill, Jane, and Bob all came.
They came with food and games.
It was good to see them.

2.

3. Tom plays ball with his mother.
Tom goes on walks with his father.
Sometimes they all read books.
Tom has fun with his mother and father.

4.

Write a title for each story that tells what it is all about.

5. ______________________________

6. ______________________________

Notes for Home: Your child identified and illustrated the main idea of two stories. ***Home Activity:*** Invite your child to name his or her favorite story. Then ask your child to tell you in a sentence or two what the story is all about.

Name ______________________________

A **verb** may tell what two or more people, animals, or things do. Do not add **-s** to these verbs.

They jog home.

Circle a word in ( ) to finish each sentence.
Draw a picture for each sentence.

1. Sal and Tim (bake/bakes).

2. Joe and Pat (plays/play).

3. The girls (jump/jumps).

4. Mom and Dad (eats/eat).

5. They (walk/walks) the dog.

Notes for Home: Your child completed sentences by choosing verbs for plural subjects. ***Home Activity:*** Write a list of verbs such as *sing, walk,* and *look*. Ask your child to use each verb in a sentence that tells about more than one person doing the action.

Name ______________________________

Pick a word from the box to finish each sentence.
Write it on the line. Use each word only once.

cousins	father	going	has	thank	very

1. Her ____________________ and mother took Jill on a trip.

2. They went to see all of her ____________________ .

3. She ____________________ a lot to tell them.

4. Jill had a ____________________ good time.

5. She is ____________________ to see them again.

6. Jill calls to ____________________ them for the fun day.

Notes for Home: Your child completed sentences using words that he or she learned this week. ***Home Activity:*** Work with your child to write a story about a family gathering using as many of these words as possible.

Name ______________________

Pick a word from the box to match each picture.
Write it on the line.

lake	cane	plane	frame	face	cage	scale	snake

1. 

2. 

3. 

4. 

5. 

6. 

7. 

8. 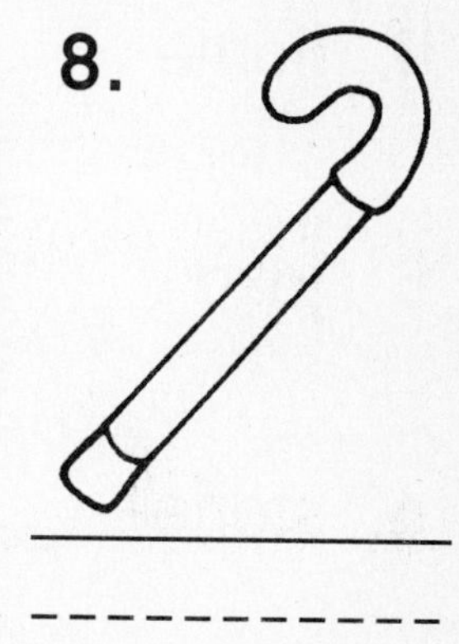

Find the word that has the same vowel sound as .
Mark the ⬭ to show your answer.

9. ⬭ tap
⬭ tape
⬭ trap

10. ⬭ plan
⬭ place
⬭ pan

Notes for Home: Your child reviewed words with the long *a* sound as in *grapes.* ***Home Activity:*** Write *face* on a sheet of paper. Have your child change the consonant letters to write a new long *a* word, such as *place.* Continue changing letters and building new words.

Name ______________________

Look at each word. **Say** it.
Listen for the **long o** sound in 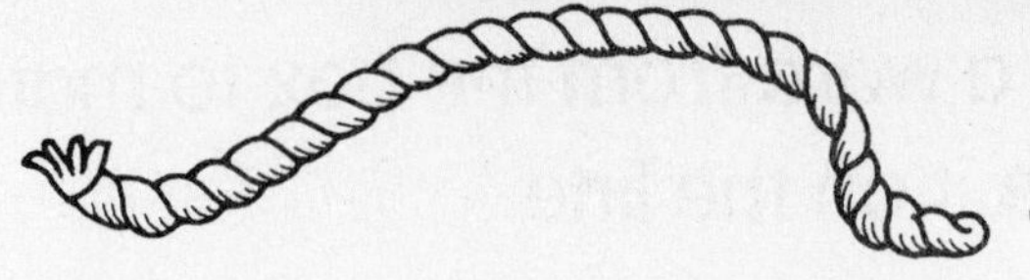 .

	Write each word.	**Check** it.
1. rode		
2. those		
3. hope		
4. home		
5. joke		
6. stone		

Word Wall Words

Write each word.

7. has		
8. very		

Notes for Home: Your child spelled words with the long *o* sound spelled consonant-vowel-consonant-*e* (CVC*e*) as in *rope,* and two frequently-used words: *has, very.* ***Home Activity:*** Challenge your child to spell other long *o* words that follow a CVC*e* pattern.

Name ______________________________

Circle the verb that tells what more than one person does.
Write the verb on the line to finish each sentence.

play plays

1. The girls ______________ a game.

runs run

2. Kim and Jill ______________ away.

hides hide

3. They ______________ in a bush.

need needs

4. They ______________ more players.

asks ask

5. They ______________ Ken and Bill to play too.

Notes for Home: Your child chose verbs to show the action of two or more people. ***Home Activity:*** Have your child tell you a story about the children in his or her class. Encourage your child to use plural subjects (two or more people) as he or she tells the story.

Name ____________________

Test-Taking Tips

1. Write your name on the test.
2. Read each question twice.
3. Read all the answer choices for the question.
4. Mark your answer carefully.
5. Check your answer.

Name ______________________________

Part 1: Vocabulary

Read each sentence.

Mark the ⊂⊃ for the word that fits.

1. This is my ______ .

⊂⊃ something ⊂⊃ father ⊂⊃ mother

2. He is ______ to get a pet.

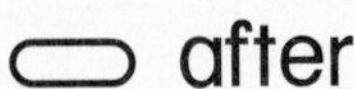

⊂⊃ after ⊂⊃ made ⊂⊃ going

3. Dad ______ a dog for me.

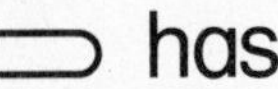
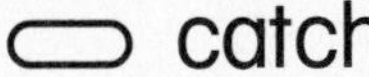

⊂⊃ has ⊂⊃ catch ⊂⊃ was

4. I am ______ happy.

⊂⊃ as ⊂⊃ every ⊂⊃ very

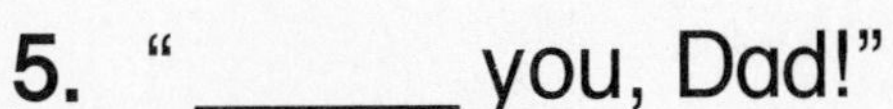
5. "______ you, Dad!"

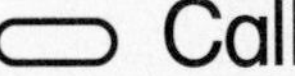

⊂⊃ Laugh ⊂⊃ Call ⊂⊃ Thank

GO ON

Name ______________________

Part 2: Comprehension

Read each question.

Mark the ⊂⊃ for the answer.

6. Where was the get-together?
   - ⊂⊃ Uncle Eddie's
   - ⊂⊃ Uncle Richard's
   - ⊂⊃ Grandma's

7. What did all the family do?
   - ⊂⊃ had fun
   - ⊂⊃ came by car
   - ⊂⊃ went up a tree

8. What is on a family tree?
   - ⊂⊃ frogs
   - ⊂⊃ jokes
   - ⊂⊃ names

9. How old was the boy who tells what happened?
   - ⊂⊃ three
   - ⊂⊃ six
   - ⊂⊃ ten

10. The boy tells mostly about
    - ⊂⊃ frogs.
    - ⊂⊃ a picture.
    - ⊂⊃ a family.

STOP

Name ______________________________

Pick a contraction from the box to finish each sentence.
Write it on the line. Remember to use capital letters.

he is = he's   she is = she's
they are = they're   they will = they'll

1. ____________________ reading a book.

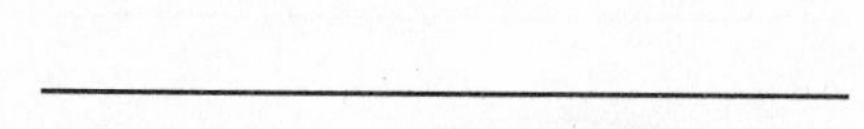

2. ____________________ asking Gram to play.

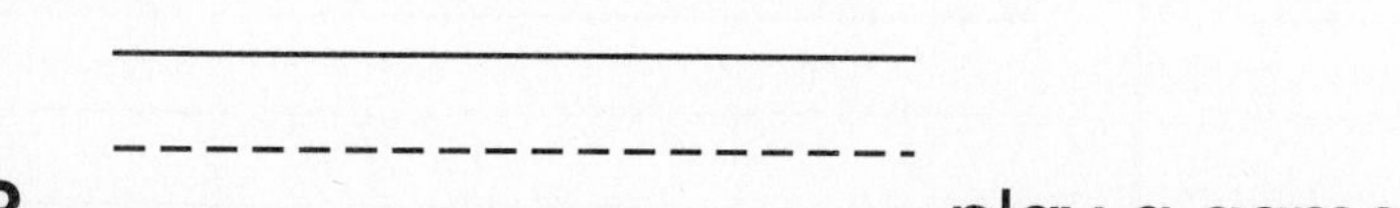

3. ____________________ play a game.

4. ____________________ having fun!

Find the contraction for the two words.
Mark the ⊂⊃ to show your answer.

5. do not
- ⊂⊃ don't
- ⊂⊃ won't
- ⊂⊃ does

6. we are
- ⊂⊃ we'll
- ⊂⊃ we'd
- ⊂⊃ we're

Notes for Home: Your child wrote contractions to finish sentences. ***Home Activity:*** Say two words that could be joined together to make a contraction. Ask your child to name the contraction and use it in a sentence.

Name ______________________

Say the word for each picture.
Pick a word from the box that rhymes with it.
Write the word on the line.

rode	those	hope	home	joke	stone

1. ______________

2. ______________

3. ______________

4. ______________

5. ______________

6. ______________

Put the letters in the correct order to make a word from the box.
Write it on the line.

has	very

7. sha ______________

8. yvre ______________

Notes for Home: Your child spelled words with long *o* that follow a consonant-vowel-consonant-*e* pattern *(rope)* and two frequently used words: *has, very.* ***Home Activity:*** Write *rope*. Have your child tell what letters to change to form different spelling words, such as *hope*.

You are your child's first and best teacher!

Here are ways to help your child practice skills while having fun!

Day 1 List some long *i* words that follow a consonant-vowel-consonant-*e* pattern, such as *rice* and *dine*. Take turns using them in sentences, for example: *The nice mice ate rice.*

Day 2 Ask your child to write or say sentences about his or her friends using any of the following words your child is learning to read this week: *be, friend, pretty, soon,* and *your*.

Day 3 Before reading a story, browse through the illustrations and some of the words together. Ask your child to use these clues to predict what the story will be about.

Day 4 Your child is learning about making introductions. Encourage your child to practice introducing himself or herself to you.

Day 5 Ask your child to tell about a family vacation or special trip that happened in the past. Listen for the use of past tense verbs. Ask questions that will help your child correct any errors using past tense verbs.

Read with your child EVERY DAY!

(fold here)

Family Times

The Rolling Rice Cake — **The Rat and the Cat**

I Like Yummy Food!

This yummy pizza looks so nice.
Please, may I have a little slice?
I'll wipe my mouth after my first bite.
I'll wipe my hands. I am polite.
I like the cherry cake surprise.
I want a slice that is just my size.
I like yogurt and an apple slice.
I'll eat a ripe melon or some rice.
I'll pack a muffin for my hike.
Then I will go and ride my bike.

This rhyme includes words your child is working with in school: words with the long *i* sound that follow a consonant-vowel-consonant-*e* pattern *(nice, bite)* and words with single or double consonants in the middle *(melon, pizza)*. Sing "I Like Yummy Food" together and act out the lyrics.

Name: ______________________

Spin It

Materials paper, paper clip, pencil, marker, 1 button per player

Game Directions

1. Make a simple spinner as shown. Players place buttons on Start.

2. Take turns spinning. Move forward that number of spaces on the gameboard.

3. Read the word in the space. If you can name another word that has the same middle consonant sound as the word in the space, spin an extra turn. For example: *ne_v_er* and *ri_v_er*.

4. The first player to reach the end wins!

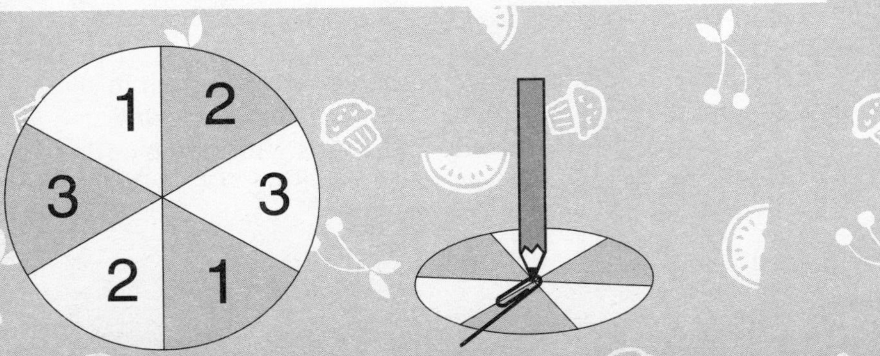

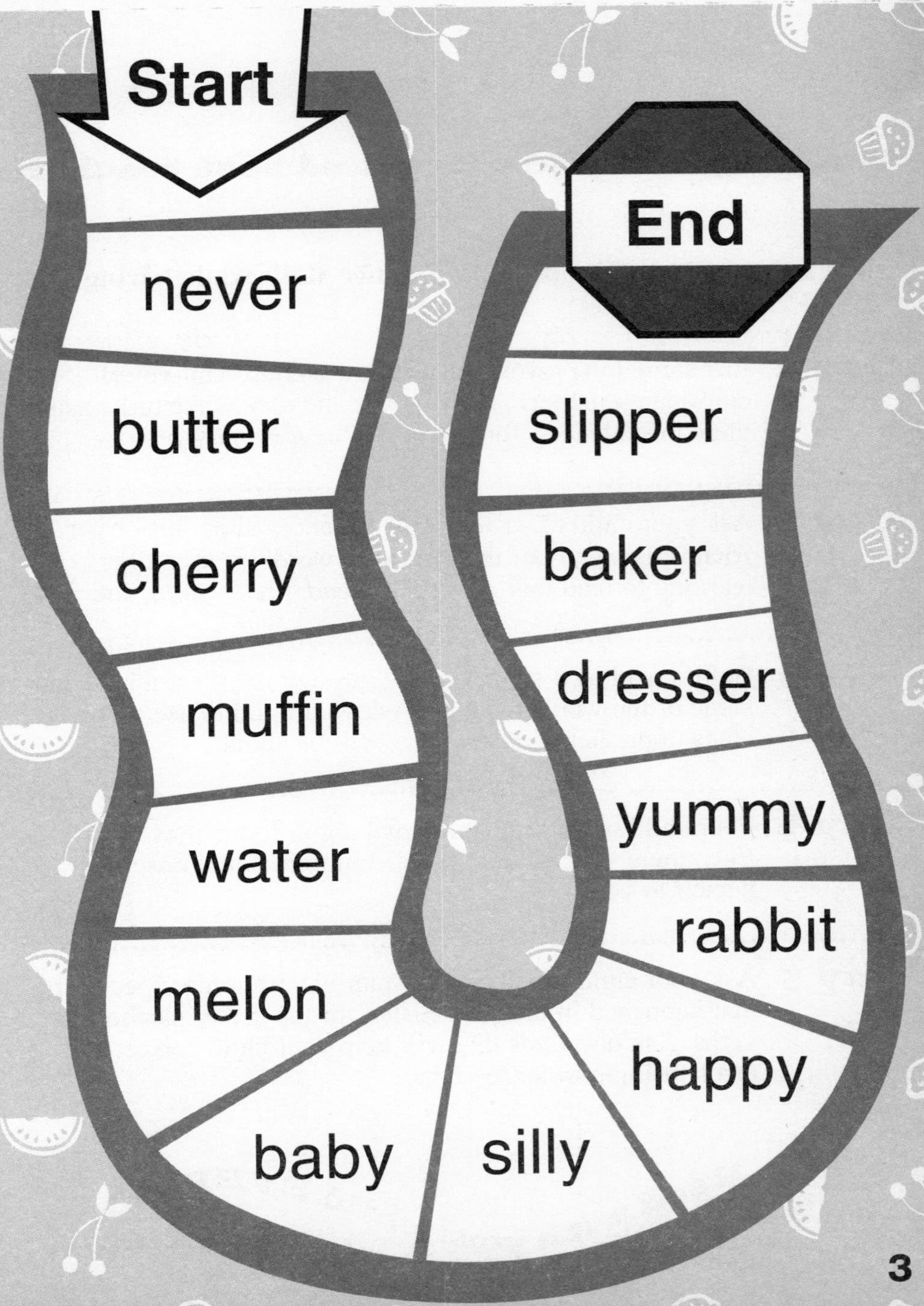

Start

never

butter

cherry

muffin

water

melon

baby

silly

happy

rabbit

yummy

dresser

baker

slipper

End

Name ______________________________

Pick a word from the box to match each picture.
Write the word on the line.
Circle each picture whose name has the **long i** sound.

bike	dime	fire	line
mice	pig	six	slide

kite

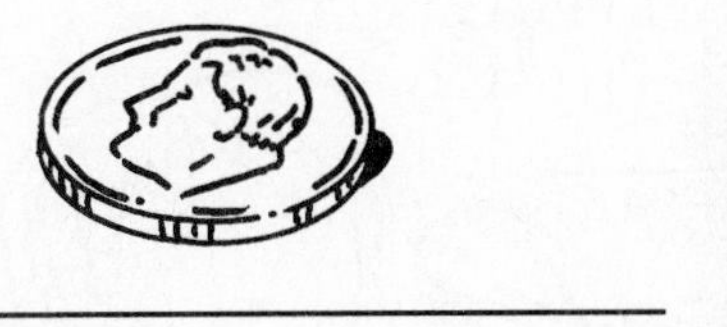

1. ______________________

2. ______________________

3. ______________________

4. ______________________

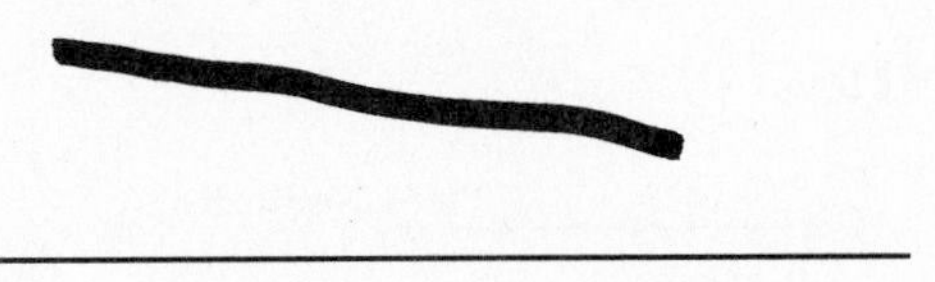

5. ______________________

6. ______________________

7. ______________________

8. ______________________

Notes for Home: Your child practiced reading words with the long *i* sound that follow a consonant-vowel-consonant-*e* pattern such as *kite*. ***Home Activity:*** Work with your child to write a story using as many of the long *i* words listed above as possible.

Name ______________________________

Pick a letter or letters from the box to finish each word.
Write the letters on the lines.

1. Tess is ha ________ y when she eats with Sid.

2. They like to eat mu ________ ins.

3. Yellow muffins are made from le ________ ons.

4. They like muffins be ________ er than cake.

5. They can ne ________ er have too many muffins!

Notes for Home: Your child completed words with single and double consonants in the middle, such as *water* and *butter*. ***Home Activity:*** List some of your family's favorite foods. Ask your child to identify the middle consonant sounds in the words.

Name ______________________

Pick a word from the box to finish each sentence.
Write it on the line.

be	friend	pretty	soon	your

1. Sal is my best ______________ .

2. She has a ______________ doll.

3. This hat is for ______________ doll.

4. It will be dark ______________ .

5. Then it will ______________ time to go.

Notes for Home: This week your child learned to read the words *be*, *friend*, *pretty*, *soon*, and *your*. ***Home Activity:*** Write these words on slips of paper and have your child practice reading each word you show.

Name ______________________________

Look at this book cover.
Circle or **write** your answers.

1. Who wrote this book? ______________________________

2. What do you think this book will be about?
   real dogs   silly dogs   a real trip

3. What do you think this book will be like?
   funny   sad   full of facts

4. Why do you think the writer wrote this book?
   to tell facts about dogs   to make you sad   to make you laugh

5. Would you want to read this book? Why or why not?

____

____

Notes for Home: Your child answered questions about why an author may have written a story. ***Home Activity:*** Before reading a story with your child, ask questions like the ones on this page to help your child think about the author's purpose for writing it.

Name ______________________________

Verbs can tell about action that takes place now.

Today Mom and I <u>cook</u> dinner.

Verbs can tell about action that happened in the past.
Add **-ed** to these verbs.

Yesterday Dad and Sam <u>cooked</u> dinner.

Look at the picture.
Circle the sentence that tells when the action happened.

1. We fix the bike.
   We fixed the bike.

---

2. We bake a cake.
   We baked a cake.

---

3. Ted and Ned jump on the bed.
   Ted and Ned jumped on the bed.

---

4. Pat and Jane water the plants.
   Pat and Jane watered the plants.

Draw a picture about the sentence.

5. Tim and Nan play in the sandbox.

Notes for Home: Your child used pictures to distinguish between present and past tense verbs in sentences. ***Home Activity:*** Write *bake, baked, mix,* and *mixed*. Work with your child to think of a sentence for each word.

Name ______________________________

Pick a word from the box to finish each sentence.
Write it on the line.

alone	be	friend
pretty	soon	your

1. Where will you eat ______________ lunch?

2. Matt eats his lunch ______________ .

3. Matt will ______________ happy to play after lunch.

4. He will play as ______________ as he can.

5. Matt likes to play with his ______________ Fran.

6. Fran has a ______________ dress.

Notes for Home: Your child used newly learned words in sentences. ***Home Activity:*** Ask your child to write simple sentences in which vocabulary words are missing. Then you fill in the missing words, and ask your child to check your answers.

Name ______________________

chick ship thorn whip

Say the word for each picture.
Write ch, sh, th, or **wh** to finish each word.

1. ______ op
2. ______ in
3. ______ ips
4. ______ eck
5. ______ ale
6. ______ ink
7. ______ irt
8. ______ umb

Find the word that has the same beginning sound as the picture.
Mark the ⬭ to show your answer.

9. ⬭ chin
⬭ shin
⬭ thin

10. ⬭ chest
⬭ shorts
⬭ why

Notes for Home: Your child reviewed words that begin with *ch, sh, th,* and *wh*.
Home Activity: Choose one of these letter combinations. Take turns with your child naming as many words beginning with that sound as you can.

Name ______________________

Look at each word. **Say** it.
Listen for the **long i** sound in  .

	Write each word.	**Check** it.
1. like		
2. nice		
3. time		
4. ride		
5. white		
6. five		

Word Wall Words

Write each word.

7. your		
8. friend		

Notes for Home: Your child spelled words with the long *i* sound heard in *bike* and two frequently used words: *your, friend*. ***Home Activity:*** Have your child tell you sentences using each spelling word. Write the sentences, leaving a blank space for each spelling word for your child to fill in.

Name ________________________

Fill in the table.
Write the words on the lines.

Now	In the Past
1. jump	________
2. walk	________
3. ________	laughed
4. ________	thanked

Circle the verb that makes sense in each sentence.
Write it on the line.

ask asked

5. Last week, we ________ Tim to come see us.

says said

6. He ________ he had to check with his dad.

have had

7. Now, we play and ________ fun.

Notes for Home: Your child wrote present and past tense verbs to complete sentences. ***Home Activity:*** Say a sentence about something happening now. Then ask your child to repeat the sentence using the past tense of the verb.

Name ______________________________

Test-Taking Tips

1. Write your name on the test.

2. Read each question twice.

3. Read all the answer choices for the question.

4. Mark your answer carefully.

5. Check your answer.

Name ______________________________

Part I: Vocabulary

Read each sentence.
Mark the ⬭ for the word that fits.

1. It is a _____ day.

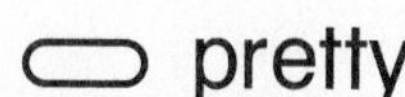

⬭ now ⬭ pretty ⬭ some

---

2. He will eat ______.

⬭ so ⬭ our ⬭ soon

---

3. A ______ comes by.

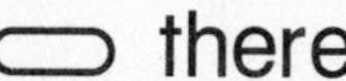
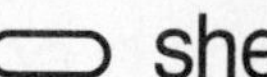

⬭ friend ⬭ there ⬭ she

4. "Is that ______ dog?"

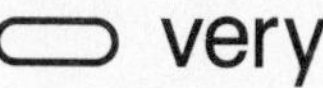
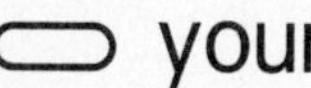

⬭ very ⬭ your ⬭ me

5. She will ______ good now.

⬭ into ⬭ there ⬭ be

GO ON

Name ______________________

Part 2: Comprehension

Read each question.

Mark the ⬭ for the answer.

6. The rat first sees the cat in
   - ⬭ a shop.
   - ⬭ a box.
   - ⬭ his home.

7. The rat wants the cat to
   - ⬭ do some tricks.
   - ⬭ be his friend.
   - ⬭ catch fish for him.

8. The man thinks the cat will
   - ⬭ run away from the rat.
   - ⬭ eat the rat.
   - ⬭ have fun with the rat.

9. What part of this story could be real?
   - ⬭ A rat has a cat for a pet.
   - ⬭ A cat talks.
   - ⬭ A man has a shop.

10. At the end, this story
    - ⬭ makes you sad.
    - ⬭ sings a song.
    - ⬭ has a surprise.

STOP

Name ______________________________

Pick a word from the box to match each picture.
Write it on the line.
Circle the picture if the **c** in the word has the same sound as in the beginning of **circle**.

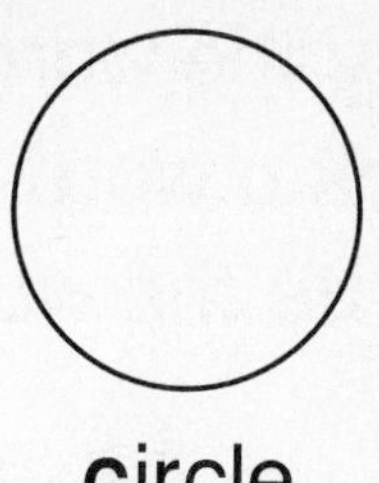

circle

cap cake car cent city face ice mice

1. ____________

2. ____________

3. ____________

4. ____________

5. ____________

6. ____________

7. ____________

8. ____________

Find the word where **c** has the same sound as in **cent**.
Mark the ⬭ to show your answer.

9. ⬭ nice
⬭ nick
⬭ sick

10. ⬭ cape
⬭ lace
⬭ lock

Notes for Home: Your child reviewed words where the letter *c* represents the sound /s/ as in *cent. **Home Activity:*** Ask your child to say a sentence that uses a word with *c* where *c* stands for the sound /s/.

Name ______________________

Say the word for each picture.
Pick a word from the box that rhymes with it.
Write the word on the line.

like nice time ride white five

1. ______________________

2. ______________________

3. ______________________

4. ______________________

5. ______________________

6. ______________________

Pick a word from the box to finish each sentence.
Write it on the line.

your friend

7. Is this ______________ bike?

8. I want to play with my ______________ .

Notes for Home: Your child spelled words with long *i* and two frequently used words: *your, friend.* ***Home Activity:*** Say a spelling word aloud. Ask your child to spell the word and then name other words that rhyme with the spelling word.

You are your child's first and best teacher!

Here are ways to help your child practice skills while having fun!

Day 1 Write the word *mule.* Challenge your child to make new long *u* words by substituting other letters for *m* and/or *l*. For example, *mule* becomes *flute* or *Luke.*

Day 2 Work with your child to make up short riddles using any of these words: *four, funny, long, watch,* and *were.* For example: *I have four fingers and one thumb. What am I? (a hand)*

Day 3 After you have read a story to your child, have your child describe the beginning, middle, and end of the story.

Day 4 Your child is learning to listen for details. Describe something using as many details as possible. Challenge your child to guess what you are describing.

Day 5 Ask your child to look at a picture and describe it by using simple sentences that include the words *is, are, was,* and *were.* For example: *He is running. They are eating.*

(fold here)

Family Times

June and the Mule **Slim, Luke, and the Mules**

The Dude Ranch

We're at the dude ranch.
We'll ride the big mules.
We'll brush them
And feed them
And follow the rules.

When it is lunch time,
We'll hear a bell ring.
We'll rush to the table
And eat everything.

Later this evening
On this cool night in June,
We'll stretch by the fire
And sing a nice tune.

This rhyme includes words your child is working with in school: words with the long *u* sound *(dude, tune)* and words that end with *ch, tch, sh,* and *ng*. Sing "The Dude Ranch" together. Underline the words with the long *u* sound and circle the words that end with *ch, tch, sh,* and *ng*.

Name: ______________________

It's a Match

Materials index cards, markers

Game Directions

1. Make a picture card and a word card for these words: *ranch, lunch, wing, watch, long, fish, brush, math, bath, ditch.* Mix each set of cards and place each card in the set facedown.

2. Players take turns turning over two cards at a time, one card from each set.

3. If the word and picture cards match, the player keeps the pair. If not, the player mixes the cards back into each set.

4. Play until all cards have been matched up. The player with the most pairs wins!

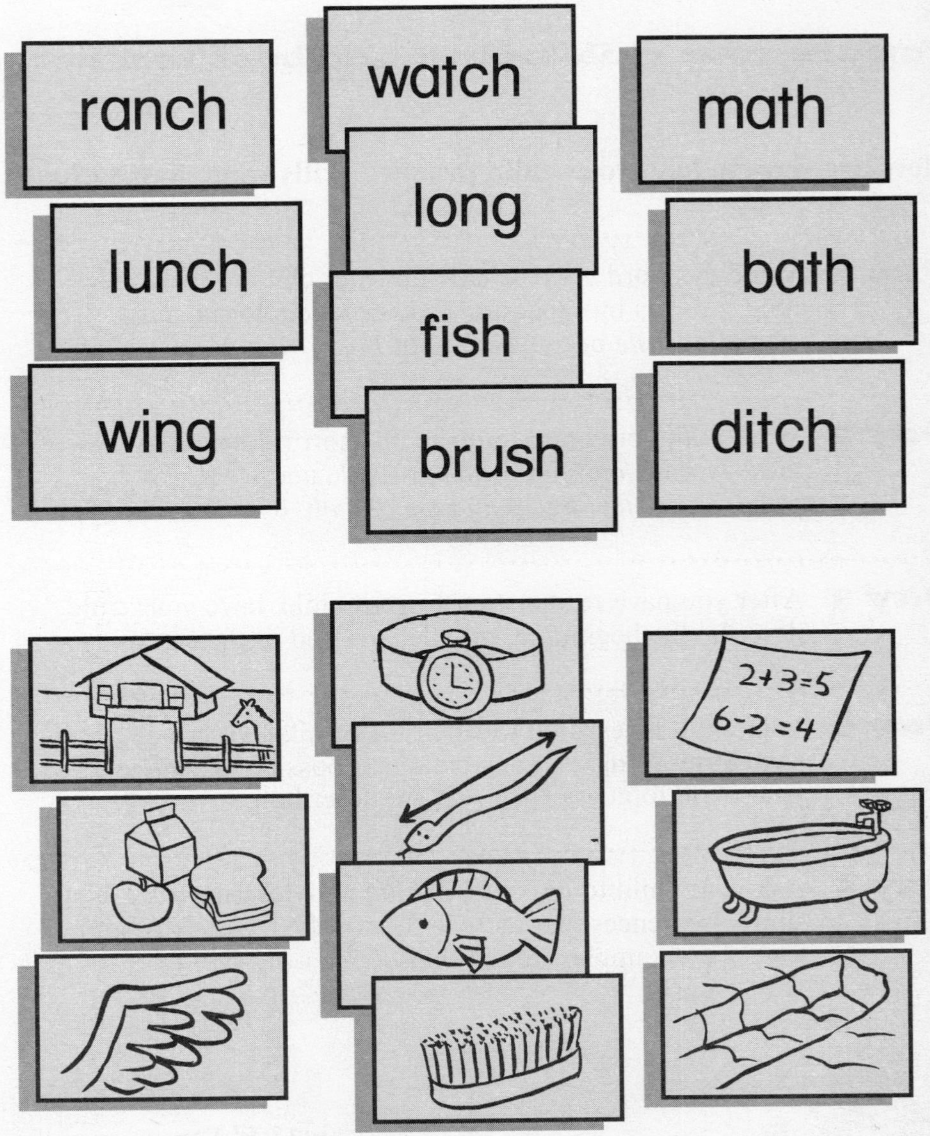

ranch
lunch
wing
watch
long
fish
brush
math
bath
ditch

2+3=5
6-2=4

Name ______________________________

Look at each picture.
Circle the word to finish each sentence.
Write it on the line.

mule

flute flop flood

1. Mike plays the ______________ .

tune tub tube

2. I filled the ______________ .

team tan tune

3. Do you like that ______________ ?

cute can cut

4. My cat is very ______________ .

cub cube cab

5. This is an ice ______________ .

Notes for Home: Your child practiced reading words with the long *u* sound that follow a consonant-vowel-consonant-*e* pattern, such as *mule*. ***Home Activity:*** Work with your child to think of pairs of rhyming words that have the long *u* sound.

Name ______________________

Pick letters from the box to finish each word.
Write the letters on the line.

bench

ch tch sh th ng

1. 
pa ______

2. 
ki ______

3. 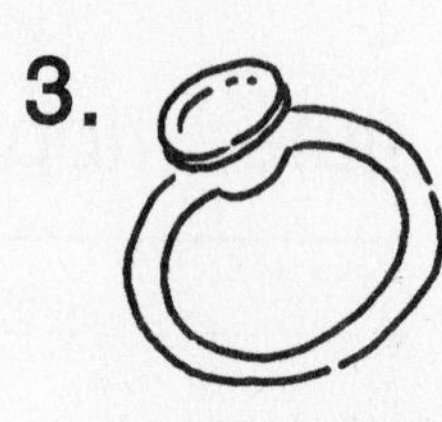
ri ______

4. 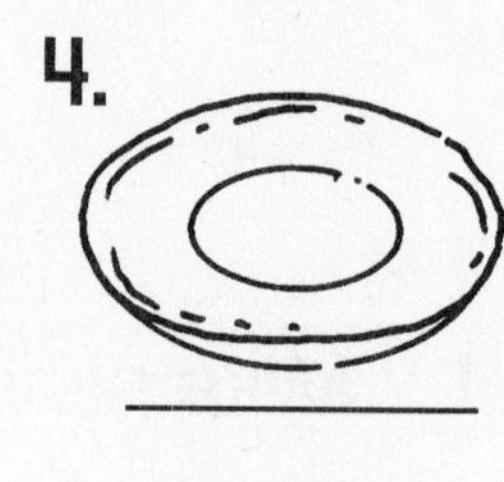
di ______

5. fi ______

6. 
lun ______

7. 

in ______

8. 
ca ______

Draw a picture for each word.

9. watch

10. moth

Notes for Home: Your child added the final digraphs *-ch*, *-tch*, *-sh*, *-th*, and *-ng* to complete words. ***Home Activity:*** Invite your child to make up sentences that include rhyming words with these endings. For example: *I wish I had a fish.*

Name ______________________________

Pick a word from the box to match each clue.
Write it on the line.

four funny long watch

1. comes after one, two, three

____

2. a _______________ rope

3. the same as *look*

____

4. the same as *silly*

____

Write a sentence using the word *were*.

5. ____

Notes for Home: This week your child learned to read the words *four*, *funny*, *long*, *watch*, and *were*. ***Home Activity:*** Challenge your child to use as many of the vocabulary words as possible in one silly sentence, such as *I watched four, long, funny clowns.*

Name ______________________________

Read the sentences in the story.
Number them from 1 to 3 to show the right order.

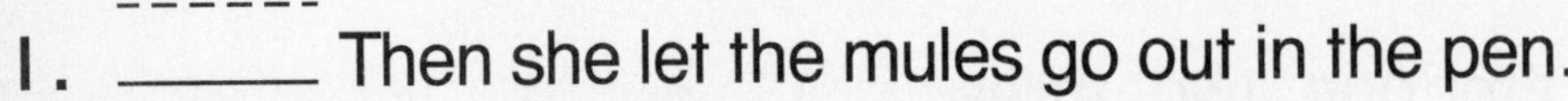

1. ______ Then she let the mules go out in the pen.

2. ______ After the mules ate, Ellen gave them water.

3. ______ Ellen fed the mules.

Draw a picture to show what happened at the **beginning.**
Draw a picture to show what happened at the **end**.

4. Beginning	**5.** End

Notes for Home: Your child numbered sentences and drew pictures to show the order of events in a story. ***Home Activity:*** Together, write a four-sentence story, with each sentence on a separate strip of paper. Help your child put the sentences in the correct order.

Name ______________________

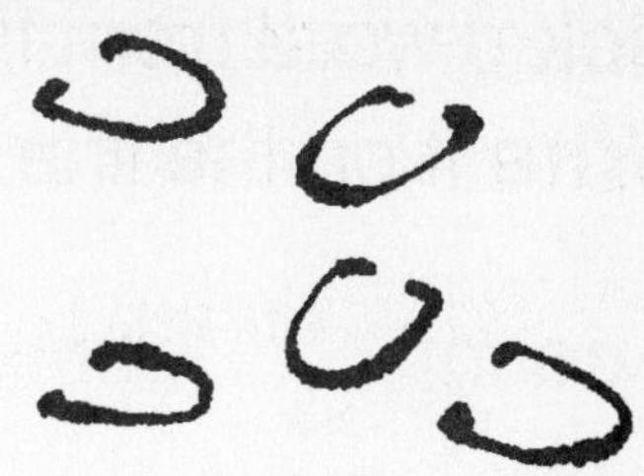

Use is and **are** to tell about now.

She **is** riding the mule.

Use was and **were** to tell about the past.

The ride **was** nice.

Write a word from the box to finish each sentence.
Use the clue in ( ) to help you.

is	are	was	were

1. He ____________ calling a friend. (now)

2. She ____________ late. (past)

3. They ____________ watching the mules. (now)

4. It ____________ nice out. (now)

5. We ____________ going home. (past)

Notes for Home: Your child used the words *is*, *are*, *was*, and *were* in sentences.
Home Activity: Write the words *he*, *she*, *it*, *we*, and *they* on slips of paper. Have your child pick one slip at a time and use each word in a sentence with *is*, *are*, *was*, or *were*.

Name ______________________________

Pick a word from the box to finish each sentence.
Write it on the line.

count	four	funny	long	watch	were

1. We ________________ going to see the mules.
2. It is a ________________ walk to the pen.
3. We like to ________________ the mules.
4. Sam will ________________ how many mules are there.
5. There are ________________ mules in the pen.
6. I laugh at the ________________ mule.

Notes for Home: Your child completed sentences using words learned this week. ***Home Activity:*** Work with your child to write a story using as many of these words as possible.

Name ______________________

This graph shows how many animals live on Jan's farm.
Read the graph.
Use the graph to answer each question.

1. How many pigs are on the farm? ______

2. How many horses and dogs are on the farm? ______

3. How many more cows are there than sheep? ______

4. What animal is there the most of? ______________

5. What animal is there the least of? ______________

Notes for Home: Your child read a bar graph and answered questions about it. ***Home Activity:*** Help your child make a bar graph that shows the number of different kinds of objects in your home. Then ask your child questions about the graph.

Name ______________________

Circle the word for each picture.

1. line lane
2. mane mice
3. kit kite
4. bike bill
5. pill pile
6. lime lame
7. fish file
8. shine shin

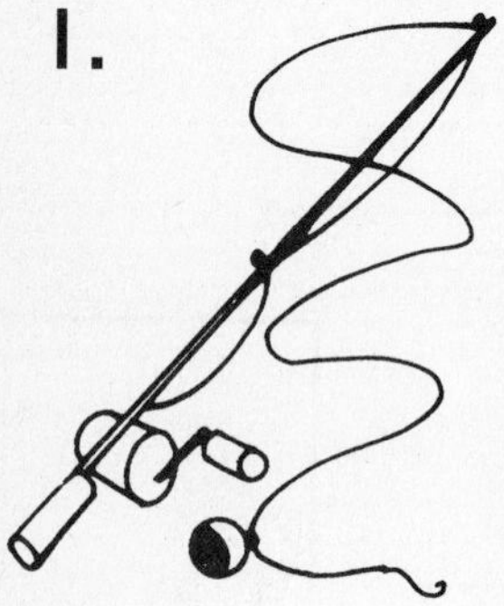

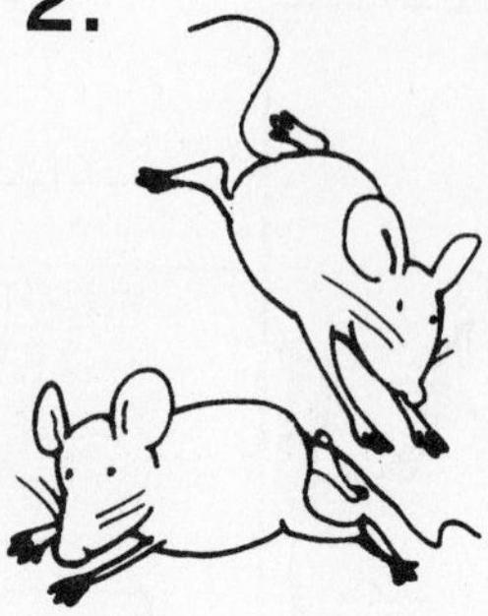

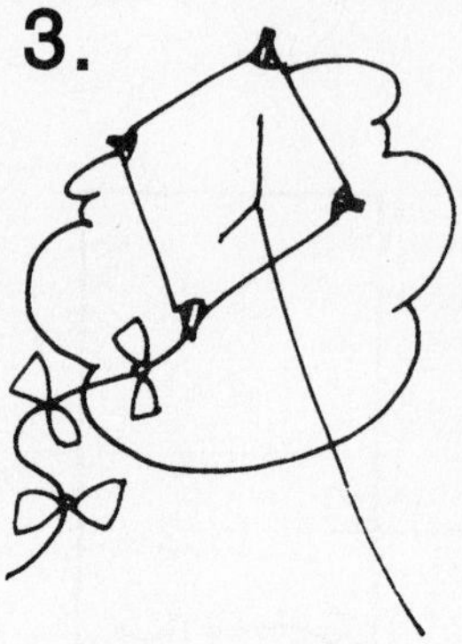

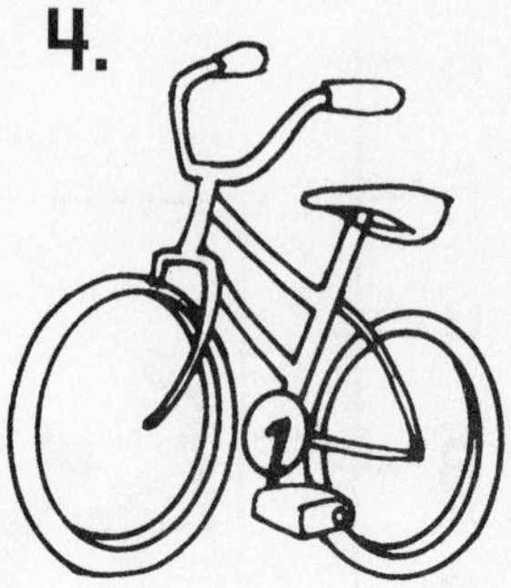

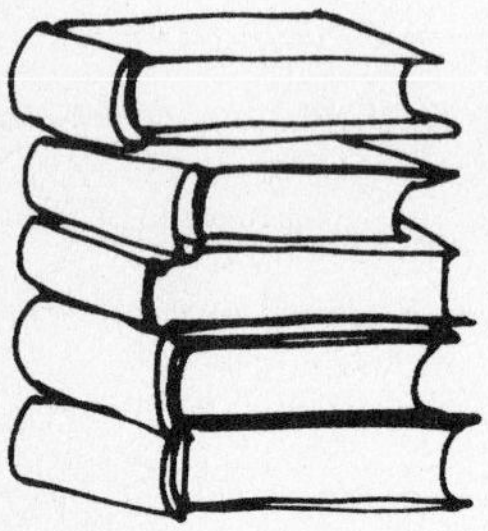

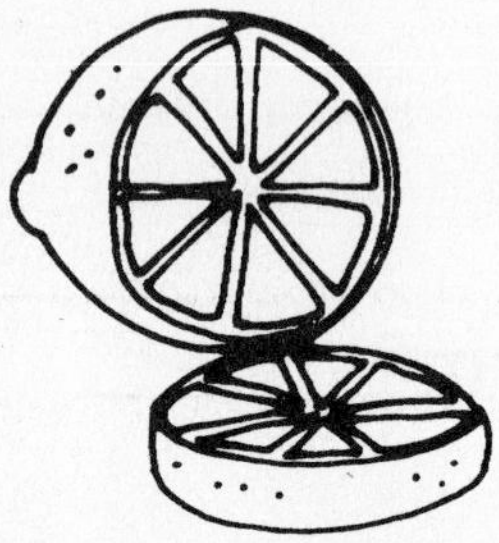

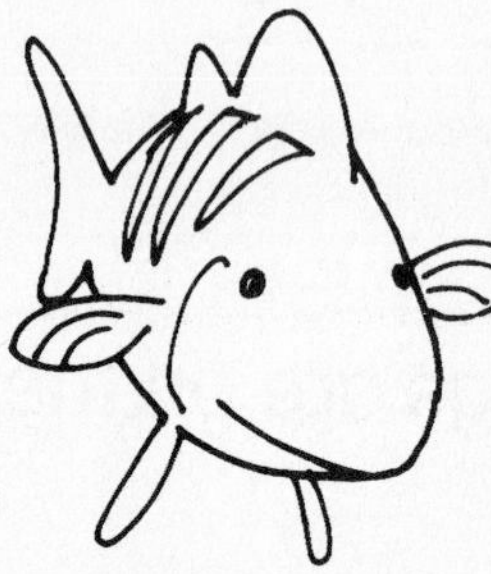

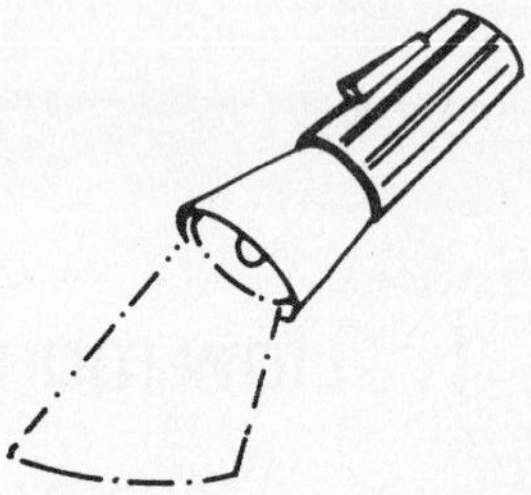

Find the word that has the same **long i** sound as .
Mark the ⬭ to show your answer.

9. ⬭ flip
   ⬭ fine
   ⬭ fin

10. ⬭ slip
    ⬭ sip
    ⬭ slice

Notes for Home: Your child reviewed words with the long *i* sound heard in *five*. ***Home Activity:*** All the long *i* words above are spelled using a consonant-vowel-consonant-*e* pattern. Write the word *five*. Take turns changing the consonants to build new words, such as *fine, dine,* and *dime.*

Name ______________________________

Look at each word. **Say** it.
Listen for the sounds that **th**, **ch**, **sh,** and **ng** stand for.

	Write each word.	**Check** it.
1. the	______________	______________
2. that	______________	______________
3. with	______________	______________
4. such	______________	______________
5. fish	______________	______________
6. long	______________	______________

Word Wall Words

Write each word.

7. four	______________	______________
8. were	______________	______________

Notes for Home: Your child spelled words with *th, ch, sh,* and *ng,* as well as two frequently used words: *four, were.* ***Home Activity:*** Help your child write a story about a fish, using these spelling words.

Name ______________________

Circle the verb that makes sense in each sentence.
Write the verb on the line.

1. Jim and Cara ____________ walking to the pen. is / are

2. Jim ____________ going to give hay to the mules. is / are

3. The mules ____________ awake. is / are

4. Before, they ____________ sleeping. was / were

5. Cara ____________ happy to give the mules water. was / were

Notes for Home: Your child completed sentences using *is*, *are*, *was*, and *were*. ***Home Activity:*** Write the words *is*, *are*, *was*, and *were* on flashcards. Have your child pick a card, read the word, and use it in a sentence.

Name ______________________________

Part I: Vocabulary

Read each sentence.
Mark the ⬭ for the word that fits.

1. There are ______ men.

⬭ four ⬭ soon ⬭ after

2. They went for a ______ ride.

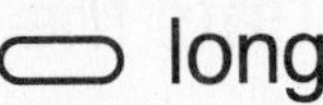

⬭ something ⬭ long ⬭ very

3. They ______ going to get some food.

⬭ has ⬭ made ⬭ were

4. One man will ______ the truck.

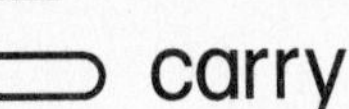

⬭ watch ⬭ carry ⬭ funny

5. He will ______ the bags.

⬭ play ⬭ count ⬭ catch

GO ON

Name ________________________________

Part 2: Comprehension

Read each sentence.

Mark the ⬭ for the answer.

6. What do Slim and Luke have to do?
   - ⬭ go to town
   - ⬭ rub down the mules
   - ⬭ work on the ranch

7. How many mules do Slim and Luke have?
   - ⬭ four
   - ⬭ five
   - ⬭ six

8. What happens when Slim counts the mules?
   - ⬭ He does not count the one he is on.
   - ⬭ A mule runs away.
   - ⬭ He counts too many.

9. What will Slim and Luke do next?
   - ⬭ go to buy food
   - ⬭ count the mules again
   - ⬭ let the mules go

10. Slim and Luke seem
    - ⬭ sad.
    - ⬭ mean.
    - ⬭ silly.

STOP

Name ______________________________

Add -ed and **-ing** to each word.
Write the new words on the lines.

	Add -ed	Add -ing
1. play		
2. rest		
3. talk		
4. help		
5. ask		

Find the word that makes sense in each sentence.
Mark the ⬭ to show your answer.

6. Now, Kit is ______ her mom.

- ⬭ called
- ⬭ call
- ⬭ calling

7. Before, Kit ______ in the park.

- ⬭ play
- ⬭ played
- ⬭ playing

Notes for Home: Your child reviewed words with *-ed* and *-ing* endings. ***Home Activity:*** Make a list of action verbs like those above. Have your child add *-ed* and *-ing* to each word and use it in a sentence.

Name ______________________

the	that	with	such	fish	long

Write three words from the box that have **th**.

1. ____________ 2. ____________ 3. ____________

Pick a word from the box to finish each sentence.
Write it on the line.

4. This is a very ____________ pole.

5. Look at the ____________ jump!

6. This is ____________ a nice pond.

Pick a word from the box to finish each sentence.
Write it in the puzzle.

four	were

7. Two plus two is ______ .

8. The boys ______ running fast.

7.

8.

Notes for Home: Your child spelled words with *th, ch, sh,* and *ng,* as well as two frequently used words: *four, were.* ***Home Activity:*** Say a spelling word aloud. Ask your child to write the word and then use it in a sentence.

You *are* your child's first *and* best teacher!

Here are ways to help your child practice skills while having fun!

Day 1 Write a list of long *e* words spelled *ee* or *e* such as *feet* and *me.* With your child, take turns thinking of sentences that tell a story. Use as many long *e* words as you can.

Day 2 Ask your child to make up sentences using these words: *about, any, ask, kind,* and *over.*

Day 3 On one side of a sheet of paper, draw a picture of something make-believe. On the other side, draw something from real-life. Ask your child to label each drawing *make-believe* or *real.*

Day 4 Your child is learning to follow oral directions. Give your child step-by-step directions for making something, such as a peanut butter and jelly sandwich. Have your child follow the directions as you say them.

Day 5 After you have read a story with your child, ask him or her to point out any contractions that are formed by joining a verb and *not (wasn't).* Have your child tell you what two words each contraction represents.

Read with your child EVERY DAY!

(fold here)

Family Times

Riddle-dee Fiddle-dee-dee — **The Riddles**

Can You Guess?

You'll see me fly
Outside by a tree.
I like to make honey.
I'm a bumblebee!

We grow very tall.
We see lots of bees.
We are very green.
We are apple trees!

We like sunshine.
We like rain showers.
We blow in the breeze.
We are tall sunflowers!

This rhyme includes words your child is working with in school: words with the long *e* sound spelled *ee* and *e (see, me)* and compound words *(outside, sunshine).* Read "Can You Guess?" aloud with your child. Put your hands in the air for each long *e* word you say.

Name: ______________________

Combining Words

Materials paper, marker, 2 coins per player

Game Directions

1. Make two large gameboards like those shown.
2. Players take turns tossing a coin onto each gameboard and reading the words in the squares where the coins land.
3. To earn a point, the two words landed on must form a compound word.
4. The first player to get 5 points wins!

snow	air	sun	in
out	some	any	every

ball	plane	shine	side
doors	body	thing	one

Name ______________________________

Help the bee get home.
Read each word.
Draw a line that only goes past the **long e** words.
Write the **long e** words on the lines.

feet
bed
beet
wet
sheet
we
net
peel
jeep
he
jet
me
Home

1. ______________
2. ______________
3. ______________
4. ______________
5. ______________
6. ______________
7. ______________
8. ______________

Notes for Home: Your child practiced reading words with the long *e* sound spelled *ee* and *e*. ***Home Activity:*** Ask your child to use the long *e* words above in sentences, such as *She gave the beet to me.*

Name ___________________________

Read each compound word.
Write the two words you see in each compound word.

snowball = snow + ball

1. cannot = __________ + __________

2. anything = __________ + __________

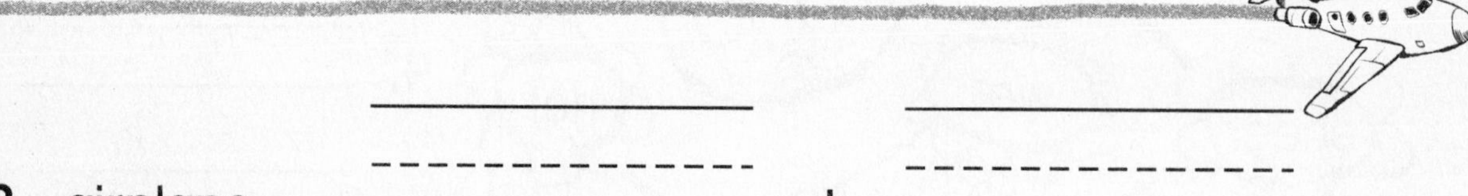

3. airplane = __________ + __________

4. inside = __________ + __________

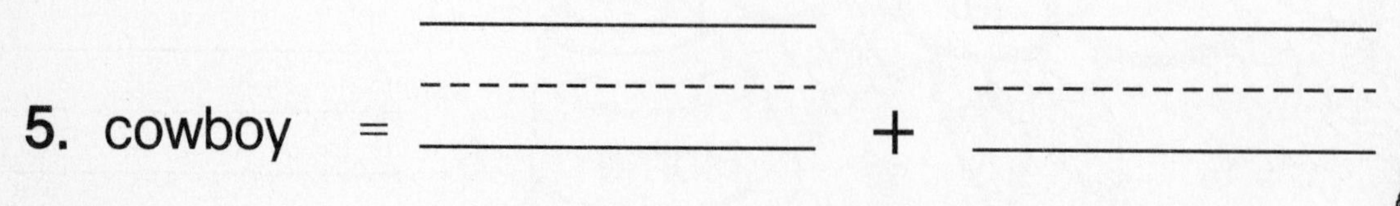

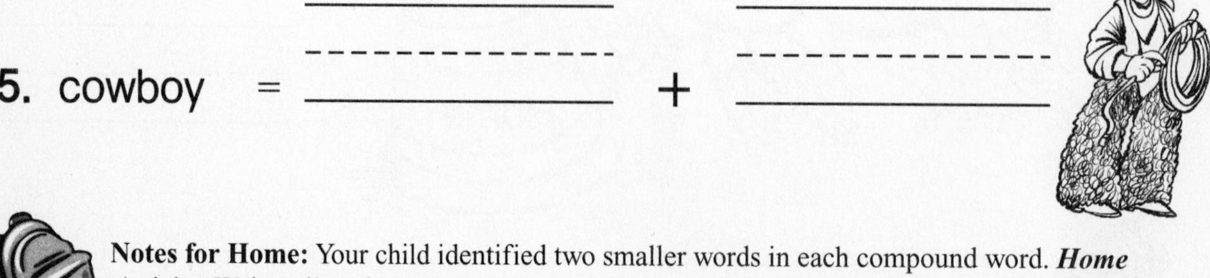

5. cowboy = __________ + __________

Notes for Home: Your child identified two smaller words in each compound word. ***Home Activity:*** Write a list of compound words. Ask your child to identify the two separate words in each compound word.

Name ______________________________

Pick a word from the box to finish each sentence.
Write it on the line.

about any ask kind over

1. Mo sees ______________ nine or ten bees.

2. Some bees fly ______________ her head.

3. Mo knows to be ______________ to the bees.

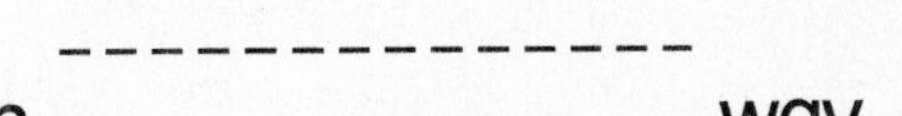

4. They do not hurt her in ______________ way.

5. Mo will ______________ her mom more about bees.

Notes for Home: This week your child learned to read the words *about*, *any*, *ask*, *kind*, and *over*. ***Home Activity:*** Write these words on slips of paper. Show each word to your child. Have him or her say the word and use it in a sentence.

Name ______________________________

Look at each picture.
Write R on the line if it could really happen.
Write M on the line if it is make-believe.

1. 

______

2. 

______

3. 

______

4. 

______

Draw a picture of something that could really happen.

5.

Notes for Home: Your child identified sentences as real or make-believe.
Home Activity: Make up a story with your child. Include parts that are both real and make-believe.

Name ______________________________

A verb and the word *not* can be put together.
They make a shorter word called a **contraction**.
The letter *o* is left out of the word *not*.
An **'** is used in place of the letter *o*.

were not = **weren't** does not = **doesn't**

Read each sentence.
Write the contraction for the underlined words.

1. Those jokes were not good. ______________

2. It is not hard to tell good jokes. ______________

3. The jokes my mom tells are not bad.

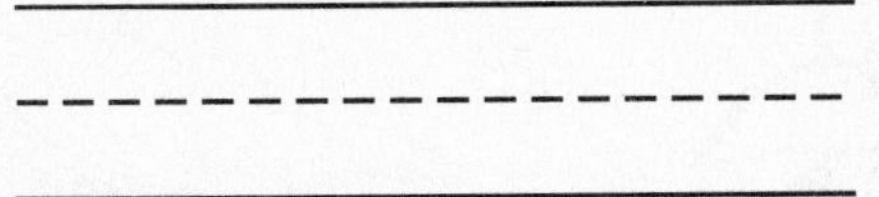

4. But my dad does not get them.

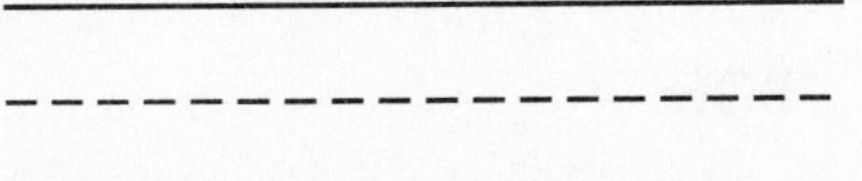

5. He was not laughing like the rest of us.

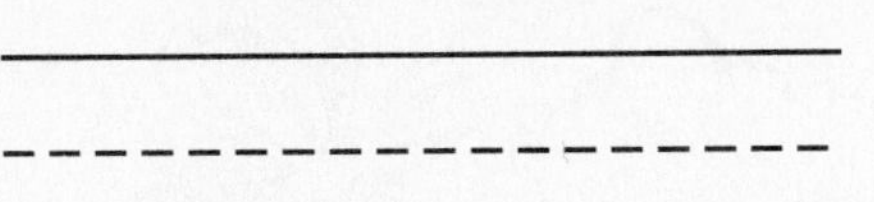

Notes for Home: Your child learned to write contractions using *not* with verbs.
Home Activity: Have your child count the number of contractions used during five minutes of family conversation. Make a list to see which contractions use *not* with verbs.

Name ______________________________

Pick a word from the box to match each clue.
Write the words in the puzzles.

about	answer	any	ask	kind	over

1. I know a riddle ______ a bird.
2. not under
3. What do you give to a question?

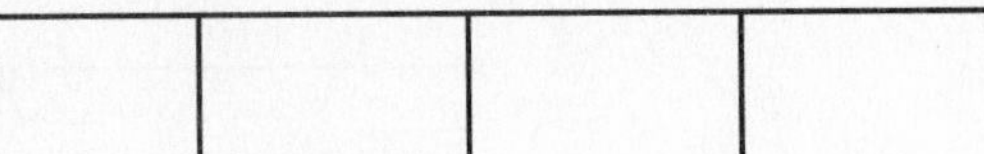

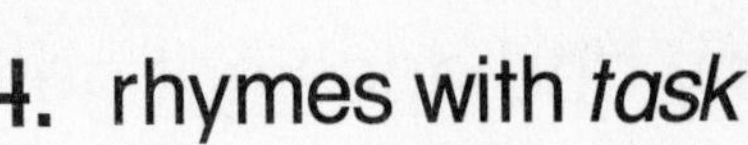

4. rhymes with *task*
5. nice
6. rhymes with *many*

Notes for Home: Your child solved puzzles using words that they learned this week.
Home Activity: Help your child write a sentence using each word.

Name ______________________________

pan bed ship pot cub

Say the word for each picture.
Write a, e, i, o, or **u** to finish each word.

1.  gr ____ n
2.  b ____ x
3.  b ____ g
4.  t ____ n
5. 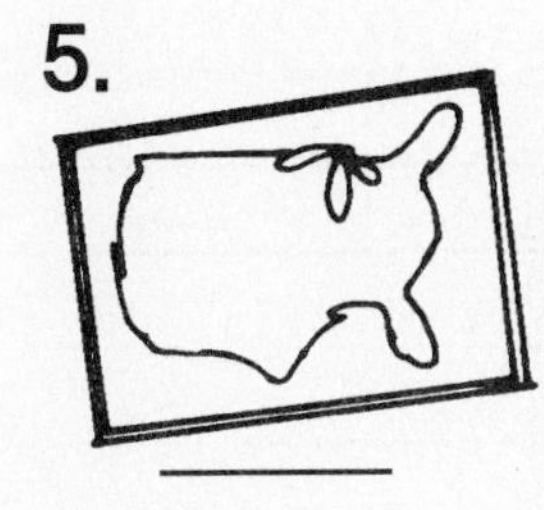 m ____ p
6.  st ____ m
7.  d ____ sh
8.  c ____ p

Find the word that has the same middle sound as the picture.
Mark the ⬭ to show your answer.

9. ⬭ dress
   ⬭ drum
   ⬭ drip

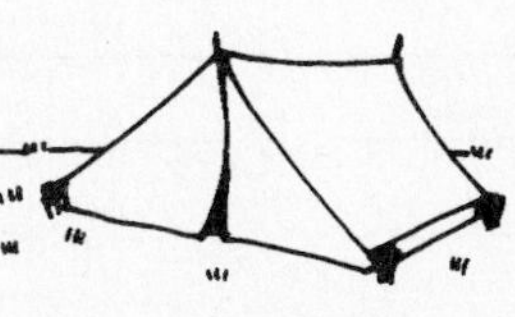

10. ⬭ pig
    ⬭ pen
    ⬭ pine

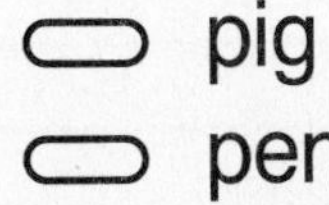
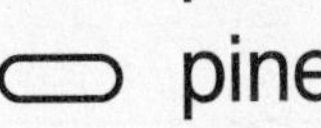

Notes for Home: Your child reviewed words with the short vowel sounds heard in *pan, bed, ship, pot,* and *cub.* ***Home Activity:*** Pick one of these short vowel words. Ask your child to name as many words as he or she can that have the same vowel sound.

Name ______________________________

Look at each word. **Say** it.
Listen for the **long e** sound in  .

	Write each word.	**Check** it.
1. we		
2. she		
3. me		
4. he		
5. see		
6. green		

Word Wall Words

Write each word.

7. any		
8. kind		

Notes for Home: Your child spelled words with the long *e* sound spelled *e* and *ee (me, see),* and two frequently used words: *any, kind.* ***Home Activity:*** Work together to write and illustrate a story about seeing a strange, green animal. Include the spelling words in the story.

Name ______________________________

Put steps in the right order.

Wrong Order	**Right Order**
She hits the ball.	He tosses the ball.
He tosses the ball.	She hits the ball.

Put these sentences in the right order.
Write them on the lines.

Drop the bat at the plate.
Swing the bat.
Pick up the bat.
Hit the ball with the bat.

1. ______________________________

2. ______________________________

3. ______________________________

4. ______________________________

Write a sentence to tell what comes next.

5. ______________________________

Notes for Home: Your child identified and wrote steps in a process in the correct order. ***Home Activity:*** Invite your child to tell you about something that he or she does that has an order—getting ready for school or a game. Ask your child to write down the steps in order.

Name ______________________________

Read each sentence.
Pick a contraction from the box to take the place of the underlined words.
Write it on the line.

aren't	didn't	doesn't	isn't	wasn't

1. Hal <u>is not</u> helping on the farm. ____________________
2. Mom and Dad <u>are not</u> happy with Hal. ____________________
3. Hal <u>does not</u> hear them call. ____________________
4. Ann <u>was not</u> home. ____________________
5. She <u>did not</u> know they needed help. ____________________

Notes for Home: Your child used *not* with verbs to make contractions. ***Home Activity:*** Write the words *is, are, was, were, do,* and *did* on flashcards. Have your child pick a card, add the word *not*, and tell you the contraction.

Name ______________________________

Part I: Vocabulary

Read each sentence.
Mark the ⬭ for the word that fits.

1. This book is _____ a dog.
⬭ soon ⬭ as ⬭ about

2. What _____ of dog is it?
⬭ kind ⬭ answer ⬭ friend

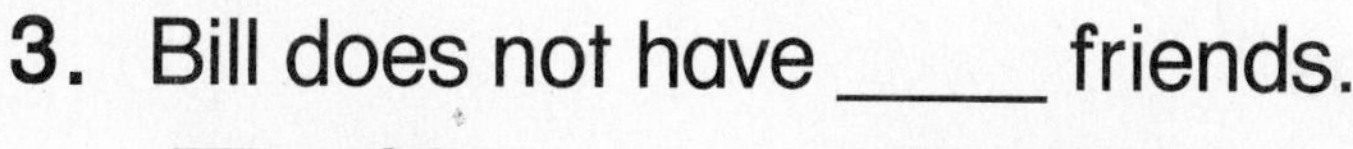

3. Bill does not have _____ friends.
⬭ very ⬭ any ⬭ for

4. I will _____ Bill to play with us.
⬭ ask ⬭ catch ⬭ bring

5. Her hat is _____ her nose.
⬭ after ⬭ some ⬭ over

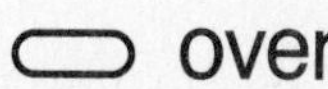
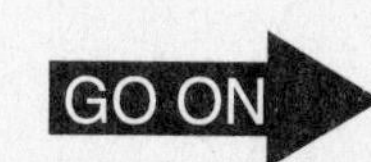

Name ______________________________

Part 2: Comprehension

Read each question.
Mark the ⬭ for the answer.

6. What is the first thing Boris wants to do?
   - ⬭ go swimming
   - ⬭ take a plane ride
   - ⬭ tell riddles

7. What does Boris do when Morris answers a riddle?
   - ⬭ laughs
   - ⬭ growls and shouts
   - ⬭ claps his hands

8. What happens when Morris tells the riddles?
   - ⬭ He makes up new answers.
   - ⬭ He won't tell the answers.
   - ⬭ He likes the answers Boris gives.

9. Why does Boris go home?
   - ⬭ to eat dinner
   - ⬭ to think up new riddles
   - ⬭ to get away from Morris

10. How can you tell this story is make-believe?
    - ⬭ A bear tells a riddle.
    - ⬭ The riddles are funny.
    - ⬭ Morris the moose has a hoof.

STOP

Name ______________________________

Circle the word for each picture.

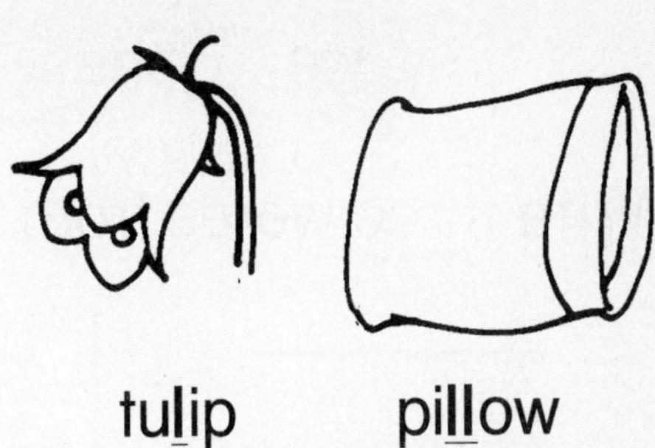

tulip pillow

1. 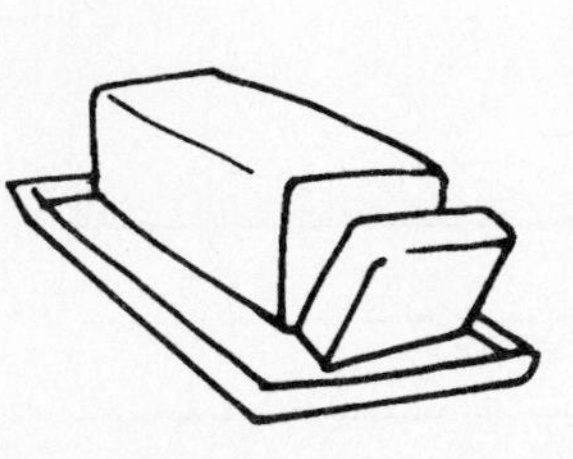
butter but

2. 
raft rabbit

3. 
carrot carpet

4. 
ladder letter

5. 
papers party

6. 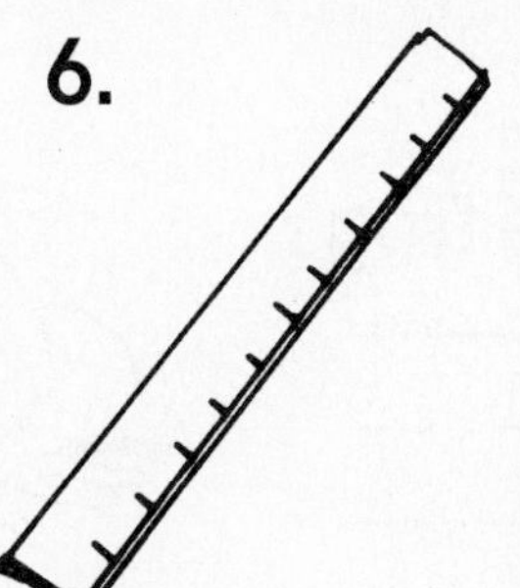
rubber ruler

7. 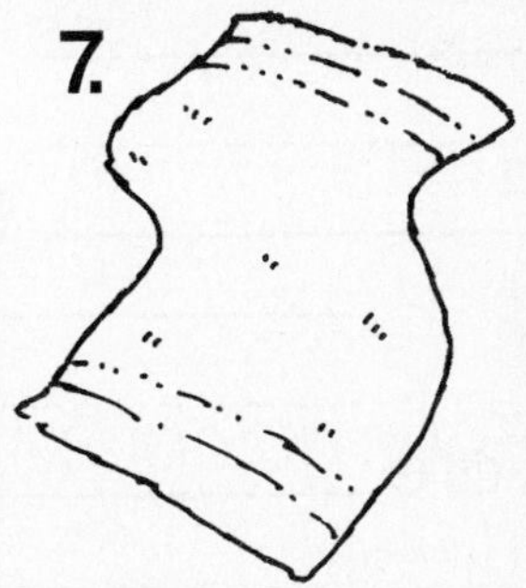
carpet card

8. 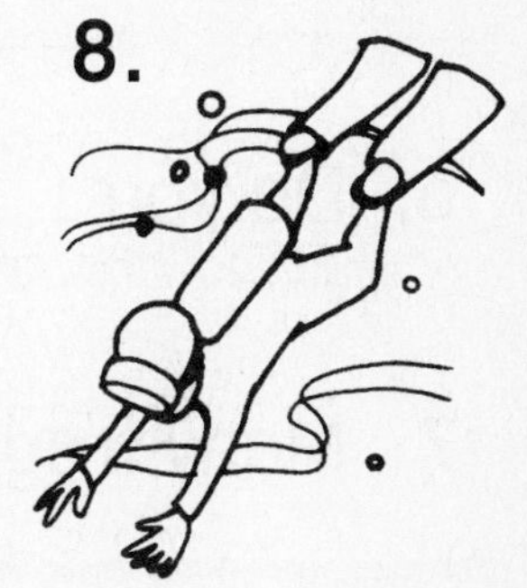
diver dinner

Find the word to match each picture.
Mark the ⬭ to show your answer.

9. ⬭ trigger
⬭ tiger
⬭ time

10. ⬭ kitten
⬭ kite
⬭ carrot

Notes for Home: Your child reviewed words with two syllables that have one or two consonants in the middle. ***Home Activity:*** Have your child choose words from the page and use each word in a sentence. Check that your child is clearly saying the middle consonant sounds.

Name ______________________

we she me he see green

Write three words from the box with just two letters.

1. ________ 2. ________ 3. ________

Write two words from the box with three letters.

4. ________ 5. ________

Pick a word from the box to finish each sentence.
Write it on the line.

6. Do you ________ the frog?

7. Many frogs are ________ .

Pick a word from the box to finish each sentence.
Write it in the puzzle.

any kind

8. Do you want ______ grapes?

9. It is ______ of you to ask me.

8.

9.

Notes for Home: Your child spelled words with the long *e* sound spelled *e* and *ee (me, see)*, as well as two frequently used words: *any, kind.* ***Home Activity:*** Have your child write the spelling words and sort them into three groups: long *e* spelled *e*, long *e* spelled *ee*, and Word Wall Words.

Name ______________________________

Correct each sentence.
Write it on the line.
Hint: Verbs that tell what one person, animal, or thing does end in **-s**.

1. Sam want to play tag.

2. Anna and Bill tells him how to play.

3. Anna run to tag Bill.

4. He laugh and run away.

5. They likes to play tag!

Notes for Home: Your child corrected verbs in sentences. ***Home Activity:*** Write action words on slips of paper, such as *jump, run,* and *play.* Take turns choosing a verb and saying sentences about one person doing the action and more than one person doing the action.

Name ______________________

I read ______________________

____

It was about

Words I Can Now Read and Write

______________ ______________

______________ ______________

Name

I read

It was about

Words I Can Now Read and Write

Name ______________________________

Words I Can Now Read and Write

Name ______________________________

I read ______________________________

____

It was about

Words I Can Now Read and Write

______________ ______________

______________ ______________

Name ____________________

Words I Can Now Read and Write

© Scott Foresman 1

Name

I read

It was about

Words I Can Now Read and Write

Name ______________________________

Words I Can Now Read and Write

Name

I read

It was about

Words I Can Now Read and Write

Name

Words I Can Now Read and Write

Name

I read

It was about

Words I Can Now Read and Write

Name

Words I Can Now Read and Write